沖縄伝統

空手・古武道の歴史

HISTORY and TRADITIONS of OKINAWAN KARATE

by Tetsuhiro Hokama

translation, editor of English version
Cezar Borkowski

editor in charge of layout
Annette Hellingrath

all photos from the
Tetsuhiro Hokama Collection

all calligraphy done by
Tetsuhiro Hokama

front cover design
Don Warrener

English editor
Marion Manzo & Michael Walsh

ISBN 0-920129-19-6

PRINTED IN CANADA

MASTERS PUBLICATION
Hamilton ● Ontario ● Canada

*"Goju Ryu Ken Shi Kai" (association founded by the author) and
"Shun Gan" (author's pen name), 1996*

About the Author

Born on the island of Formosa (now Taiwan) in 1944, Hokama Tetsuhiro (8th Dan), is a proud descendant of anji (feudal ruling class). He grew up listening to tales of martial arts folklore told to him by his great uncle and grandfather.

Hokama Sensei began his martial arts education as a teenager and almost immediately displayed impressive natural ability. Presently he studies Karate with Goju-ryu legend Higa Seikou and his top disciple Fukuchi Seiko. Matayoshi Shinpou tutored him in the art of Kobudo.

For nearly forty years Hokama Tetsuhiro has researched a broad range of martial arts. These have included virtually every style of Karate and Kobudo, as well as various methods of the native 'Ti.' This exhaustive study led him to publish *History of Okinawan Karatedo* in 1984 and five years later *Okinawan Ancient Martial Arts Tools*.

Hokama Sensei is the head of Okinawan Ken Shi Kai, a large international organization with branches in mainland Japan, South Africa, the United States and Canada. Additionally, he established the first prefectural museum of Karate-do located in Nishihara.

He is an accomplished author, curator, lecturer and calligrapher. It is his life's mission to study all martial arts and share his research with practitioners throughout the world. Hokama Sensei is to be applauded for his selfless, unswerving commitment to spreading true Okinawan Budo culture.

I have had the pleasure of knowing Hokama Tetsuhiro, often described as the 'Guardian of Okinawa's Budo Traditions,' for several years. He has served as my Okinawan guide and mentor since 1993 and honoured me with the privilege of working on the translation and publication of this - his latest book *History and Traditions of Okinawan Karate*.

- Cezar Borkowski

(A complete list of the author's accomplishments can be found at the end of this book.)

The author, Hokama Tetsuhiro.

Special Acknowledgements

Although several non-Japanese instructors have made commitments to translate and publish *History and Traditions of Okinawan Karate,* Cezar Borkowski is the individual who has spent the last year bringing this project to fruition.

Cezar Borkowski - *Senior Researcher*
Cezar Borkowski (7th Dan), is the National Director of the Northern Karate Schools which were established in 1972 in Toronto, Ontario, Canada. 2000 plus active students now train weekly in five different schools. The curriculum includes Okinawan Karate and Kobudo. Cezar Borkowski is an author, a lecturer, as well as a featured performer and colour commentator (video tapes and television). He also keeps busy as the founder and director of the Ryu Kyu No Kaze Society, an organization dedicated to the research and propagation of Okinawan martial arts.

Mr. Borkowski's research and editorial team included his colleagues Michael Walsh and Marion Manzo.

Michael Walsh - *Researcher and Editor*
Born in England, Michael Walsh (4th Dan), has resided in Canada for nearly twenty years. He is a graduate of Newcastle University with an honours degree in music education. As the Director of the Don Mills location of the Northern Karate Schools, Mr. Walsh has successfully combined his love of teaching with his passion for martial arts. He has traveled to Okinawa for the purpose of researching and editing this book. Further, to promote better understanding of Okinawan and other martial arts, Mr. Walsh has also provided assistance in the publication of numerous articles for a variety of magazines.

Marion Manzo - *Researcher and Editor*
Marion Manzo was born in New York and has lived in Canada for the past thirteen years. She is a graduate of Adelphi University (communications, magna cum laude). Ms. Manzo has more than twenty years of experience studying martial arts, initially with renowned Shotokan instructor Toyotaro Miyazaki. She was formerly a top-ranked kata competitor. Additionally Ms. Manzo, a 4th Dan, has co-directed a variety of events and co-authored numerous articles for martial arts magazines.

Acknowledgements

History and Traditions of Okinawan Karate, chronicles forty years of research. It is an investigative journey into the birth and evolution of Okinawan martial arts that could not have been accomplished without the selfless dedication of Noriko Tozawa and Kiichi Ishii, the translators of this work, as well as Professor Wally Jay.

Ongoing support, as well as several rare photographs, were provided by the International Ryukyu Karate Research Society under the direction of Patrick Mc Carthy, colleague and friend who shares my passion for the martial arts.

Additionally, I am humbly indebted to the countless men and women throughout the world who have devoted their lives to the dissemination of Okinawan culture and specifically, the propagation of Karate and Kobudo.

Finally, I would be remiss were I not to express heartfelt gratitude to my family, friends, teachers, colleagues and students. They have provided me with invaluable support for this project and all my endeavours.

Foreword

I have great respect for Karate and those who teach it. It is a Sensei's duty to hand down the Karate he has learned for posterity. The author of this book, Hokama Tetsuhiro, has researched and studied for many years with the goal of creating a work that will further our understanding of Karate.

Hokama Sensei has been a dedicated Karateka since he was a high school student. While enrolled in University, he was elected leader of the Karate club and he has continued to guide others along the way of Karate. As Mr. Hokama is a teacher, it is appropriate that he has been instrumental in the conception and realization of the *Okinawa High School Karate Championships*. Many young Karateka train vigorously in preparation for this event. It is Hokama Sensei's hope that this experience will stimulate the student to a lifelong pursuit of the martial arts.

Mr. Hokama's research and teaching assignments have taken him to Canada, the United States, Italy, France, Formosa, the Philippines, England, Mexico and Finland. Everywhere he travels, he shares his knowledge. Now, with the publication of this book, we can all benefit from the brilliant insights of Hokama Tetsuhiro.
- Joen Nakazato, 10th Dan, Hanshi, Shorinji-ryu

While the author of *History and Traditions of Okinawan Karate* Hokama Tetsuhiro, is a teacher of Goju-ryu, this is a good book for all Karate practitioners whose aim it is to cultivate a fuller understanding of their art.

Mr. Hokama is a devoted Karateka and I have had the privilege of witnessing many of his impressive demonstrations.

Hokama Sensei's reputation extends beyond the borders of Okinawa. His name is spoken with reverence in many distant countries where he is praised for his martial wisdom and knowledge. This book will be of interest to all serious martial artists.
- Uechi Kanei, 10th Dan, Hanshi, Uechi-ryu

I have known Hokama Tetsuhiro since high school and have always thought of him as an elegant scholar. I was, therefore, somewhat surprised that Karate became his chosen art, but this book is evidence that he made the right choice.

I am certain that Hokama Sensei will long remain a strong voice for Okinawan Karate.
- Kenjiro Nishida, Member of the Okinawa Prefectural Assembly

I am honoured to write a testimonial on behalf of the wonderful new book **History and Traditions of Okinawan Karate**. Hokama Sensei is a rare and talented person. He deserves to be acknowledged as an expert in all matters pertaining to the martial arts. Indeed, I count myself fortunate to call him my friend.

I am particularly excited that this book will be published in English. It is Hokama Sensei's chosen mission to preserve and promote Okinawan culture through the teaching of Karate and Kobudo throughout the world.

Mr. Hokama, an expert instructor with dedicated students training in many countries, is more than just a teacher. He is also a true Renaissance man who is as comfortable discussing philosophy or history with academics, as he is on the dojo floor.

I have known Hokama Sensei for many years and he never ceases to impress me with the dedication and sincerity he devotes to his vocation. He also possesses an enthusiasm for life that makes him entertaining and stimulating company. The work he has undertaken in his writings will leave a legacy for future generations. I am certain that through his scholarship and selfless commitment to the art he loves so dearly, he will be accorded a place in the annals of Karate history.

It is my hope that this English translation will bring the name of Hokama Tetsuhiro to a new audience, undoubtedly, they will be stimulated to further their study of Karate. In this way they will preserve the treasures of Okinawan culture that are contained in this most noble art.
- Yoshiaki Gakiya, All Okinawa Kobudo Association Head Master

I have been privileged to spend a great deal of time in the company of Hokama Sensei and I am greatly impressed by the man.

His talents are not limited to the teaching and practice of Karate. He is also a man of letters, having published several books and numerous articles, on the origin and evolution of Okinawan martial arts. It is through the efforts of men such as he, that Karate will continue to flourish and prosper as a true art form.

Hokama Tetsuhiro is, without question, destined to become a legend of the martial arts in his own right. Through diligent study and intense practice, he has established a reputation among his peers as being a man of action, constantly working on numerous projects that will result in the dissemination of Karate.

In spite of his many accomplishments and impressive intellect, Hokama Tetsuhiro remains a humble and self-effacing individual. He seeks no glory for himself. Rather, he promotes the philosophy of Karate with a view to ensuring the world will become a better place through martial arts practice.

Hokama Sensei is also a proponent of all Okinawan art forms. I can personally attest to his love for the music and dance of our beautiful island home. The calligraphy that his brush produces is strong and bold, yet sensitive - much like the man himself.

The book you now hold in your hands should be cherished, as it is the work of one of Okinawa's most creative artists. He is a man I admire and respect for the manner in which he lives his life - always giving and never expecting anything in return. It is my deepest wish that this book brings Hokama Sensei to new readers in the West. They would be well advised to understand and appreciate the task he has undertaken and to support him in his future endeavours.
- Miyazato Eiko, Kaicho, Eiruy Kai

"Action and Quiet"

Introduction

Since *History and Traditions of Okinawan Karate* made its debut in Japanese several years ago under the title *History of Okinawan Karate-do*, I have received numerous requests from martial arts practitioners regarding re-publication of this text in English.

History and Traditions of Okinawan Karate marks the culmination of my personal and professional investigation - spanning four decades - into the facts and fiction that surround the evolution of the martial arts. Furthermore, it is a celebration of the unique, wonderful culture of Okinawa.

Like other texts devoted to this subject, it contains an overview of the origins of the martial arts, profiles of Karate and Kobudo pioneers and information regarding the development of modern Budo.

Unlike other books *History and Traditions of Okinawan Karate* also contains my reflections on forty years devoted to an intensive study of a broad range of combative arts. It also offers a wealth of information in the form of interviews, photographs, calligraphy and instructional notes. The material contained herein has been assembled in a reader-friendly format utilizing minimal footnotes. Where appropriate, translated text has been edited and expanded to include additional information. The text has been organized into a primary section, focusing on theory and history, supplemented by a secondary section that contains training suggestions.

It is my sincere hope that each reader, regardless of rank or style, will find this text enlightening, entertaining and informative.

CONTENTS

すべて人々は
反撃する
技能をもつ

"Everyone has the skill to fight back."

PART ONE
Origins of Martial Arts

The Inception of Empty Hand Fighting Systems

An old Okinawan proverb tells us that - to live in the world you must be prepared to defend yourself. To be unprepared and to do so is foolish when one is faced with a hostile environment that threatens one's very existence.

Birds and animals have the ability to defend themselves; indeed, they have a reflexive response to attack. Humans share this survival instinct. They too, are well equipped to defend themselves using their limbs to yield, thrust, pierce, kick, punch, throw, twist, and push or pull, if attacked.

There is evidence that most, if not all, ancient cultures practiced some type of self-defense training. These skills were much valued in primitive times when rival groups fought each other in their struggle to exist. These were the origins of martial arts.

For centuries, the Ryukyan people have studied intensely and continually to refine their methods and techniques of self-defense called 'Ti.'[1] This system of personal defense, later infused with elements of Shorinji Kenpo of Chinese Kenpo, was handed down as an integral part of Okinawan culture. There are virtually no written records of Ti.

As a result, in examining these combative styles we are compelled to rely on oral history which tells us that present day Karate originated from ancient Okinawan fighting systems, or Ti. As with exploration of other cultural elements shared from generation to generation by word-of-mouth, one must remain open-minded when investigating the roots of Okinawan martial arts.

"The origins of 'Ti'."

---

[1]'Ti,' 'Di' and 'Te' are phonetic interpretations of the ideogram that signifies 'hand.'

15

Buddhism and the Origins of the Martial Arts

Several historians claim that the origins of the Shorinji Kenpo-style Ti can be traced back more than 1400 years when an Indian monk Dharuma or Daruma (in Indian 'Bodhidharma'[2]) traveled to China in 520 A.D. There, he established the Buddha-mind or 'Ch'an'[3] school, also referred to as 'Lanka.'

The emperor, Liang Wu Ti, had placed strong imperial support behind the propagation of Buddhism in China. He did not, however, embrace this 'Zen' (in Japanese) method which was based on the principle of 'vast emptiness.' Therefore, Dharuma retired to the Tsuzan Shorinji temple in Kanansho. There, legend has it, he meditated (zazen) by "contemplating a wall" for nine years. He also taught other monks a system of body and mind training called 'Ekkinkyo."

After Dharuma's death, while repairs were being made to the temple a box containing two books - Ekkinkyo and Senzuikyo were discovered. Many experts believe these books have had a profound effect on the development of the martial arts. For example, numerous martial arts masters contend the Ekkinkyo was later introduced to the people of the Ryukyus as 'Shorinji Kenpo' or 'Chinese Kenpo.' Ekkinkyo was synthesized with native self-defense forms to produce Okinawan Ti.

It should be noted that there are two opposing views regarding the relationship of Buddhism to

the development of martial arts. Some scholars subscribe to the school of thought that there is a strong connection between Buddhism and Chinese Kenpo.

Others, like the famous teacher Arakaki, have emphatically stated that Karate did not come from Buddhism. Instead, they are of the opinion that two martial arts, 'Shorin-ryu' and 'Shorei-ryu,' were brought from China to Okinawa. They believe that Karate was developed from these fighting systems.

"Mushin"

---

[2] Bodhidharma - translated: 'Bodhi,' meaning truth or wisdom of Buddha and 'darma' meaning law.
[3] Ch'an - in Sanskrit may be written as 'dhyana' and translated as 'meditation.'

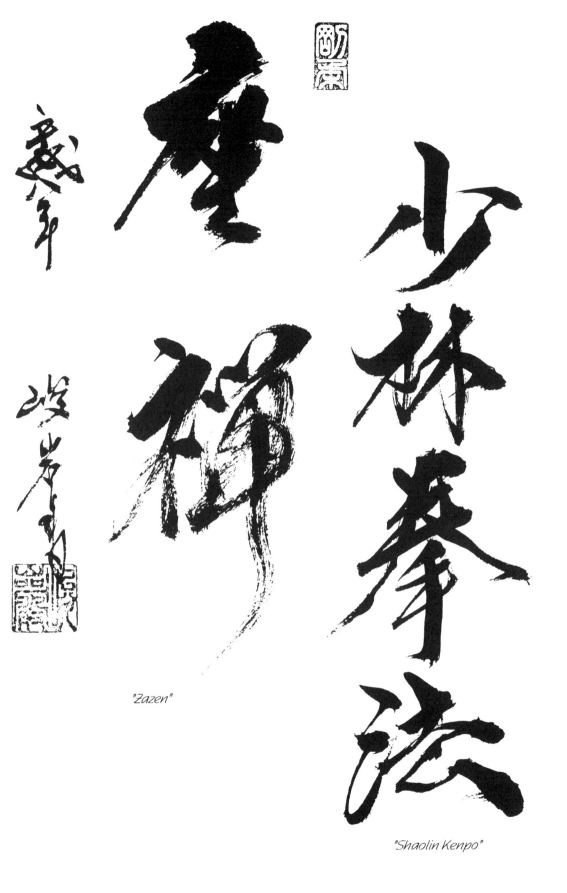

少林拳法

坐禅

"Zazen"

"Shaolin Kenpo"

17

Ekkinkyo and Senzuikyo

According to Kenko Toyama in his book *Karate-do Taikohan,* the two books written by Dharuma, Ekkinkyo and Senzuikyo, document the methods the monks taught.

They are, like their founder, heavily shrouded in mystery. Ekkinkyo (in Chinese - Yi Jin Jing translated - muscle change classic), focuses on corporal development.

Senzuikyo (Xi Sui Jing or muscle washing classic), is related to human love and desire.

The Karate expert and scholar Sato Kinbe obtained the two books and published a translation entitled *Ekkinkyogi - The Teachings of Ekkinkyo.*

Excerpts from Ekkinkyogi, which provide insight into the nature of these two books, are included in Section 1 of the Training Guide at the end of this book.

The knowledge contained in Ekkinkyo and Senzuikyo, which many scholars claim provided the foundation for Chi Kung, is relevant to both medical science and martial arts.

The former, emphasizes physical exercise to strengthen the body, and the latter, focuses on creating internal health using a prescribed method of breathing.

Buddhist priests, often credited with developing Shorinji Kenpo, employed this regimen to become healthy and strong. As such, these books are viewed as instructional manuals that enable practitioners to reap some of the many benefits associated with martial arts study.

There has been a resurgence of interest among medical practitioners, as well as the general public, in ancient healing techniques.

In keeping with this new level of interest, coupled with the Buddhist philosophy of non-violence and the inclusion of healing techniques as part of martial arts training, the following section is devoted to 'Kappo' or resuscitation procedures.

The Martial Arts as Healing Arts

It is important that readers be mindful of the fact that the purpose of Okinawan styles of fighting is to discourage or temporarily disable - rather than kill the aggressor.

The secret techniques of seizing the vital lines of the body are reserved to the advanced levels of study in certain ryuha. This same philosophy is expressed in the teaching or resuscitation techniques to advanced students of the martial arts.

If a martial artist is forced to defend himself, and in so doing, strikes the aggressor's vital point, he will render him unconscious. If he does not administer a revival technique immediately, death will usually follow swiftly.

Shindo Tenshin-ryu Kappo Hidenkai

The book *Shindo Tenshin-ryu Kappo Hidenkai* contains teachings relating to the healing aspects of the martial artist's training. The book has been preserved by the Shindo Tenshin-ryu Kenpo School and has been passed on, from generation to generation, for more than twelve hundred years.

Kappo [4] often described as first aid techniques, are explained in this most significant book. The

---

[4] With respect to Kappo teachings, there has been considerable debate regarding techniques employed in 'reviving the dead,' which may in fact, refer to resuscitation procedures used to treat unconscious patients. Rather than arguing the issue of 'dead' versus 'unconscious' patients, or attempting to dispense medical advice, the author, translator and editors are simply presenting information about Kappo for the interest of the reader.

current head of the ryuha is Ueno Takashi. Ueno Sensei learned Shindo Tenshin-ryu from his grandfather. Additionally, he studied Kenpo with several distinguished teachers including Mabuni Kanwa, Shinken Taira, Funakoshi Gichin, Motobu Choki and Yabiku Moden.

Learning Kappo

In the ancient tradition, when a master decided it was time to hand on the knowledge of Kappo, he would meditate deeply to cleanse body and mind, and invoke the God's favour to his endeavour. The teaching would be solemnly imparted to the chosen students who would have to practice repeatedly to memorize the material.

As Kappo is dependent on a strong psychological force, it must be performed with conviction. To administer Kappo, you must first achieve a heightened state of mind by focusing your spirit, breathing calmly, and drawing energy to the lower abdomen.

Once you have reached the appropriate state, quickly ascertain the cause of death. As the first action taken is crucially important, extreme care must be exercised when performing the diagnosis. Kappo will not succeed if the body has been dead for a lengthy period, nor is it guaranteed to revive all patients more recently deceased.

The most accurate method to determine if Kappo will help is to lie the body on its back and place your ear to the lower left part of the chest. Listen for a faint, regular pumping, rather than a pronounced heartbeat. Remain still and should you detect this sound, perform Kappo.

Dangers of Kappo

If you have occasion to perform Kappo on a person who attacked you and may be aware of your knowledge of the martial arts, exercise extreme caution. The assailant may be feigning death and might counter-attack as you approach to revive them.

Shift the 'dead' body so that it is lying on its back. Be very careful, dead weight is heavy and should be moved slowly and gently. Hold from behind, lifting under the arms to obtain the required position. Massage the body as if you were gathering energy towards the lower abdomen.

Observe closely for any of the following signs of life:

(1) If the pupils of the eyes are clear there is a possibility of revival.

(2) In the case of a drowning victim, it is necessary to check the colour of the fingernails first, if the nails still remain a red or pink hue, the victim may be saved by Kappo techniques.

(3) Facial colour is a good indicator of the possibility of saving a drowned subject. In the case of an accidental drowning, the victim's face will retain a red tone which indicates a good chance of saving their life.

(4) In case of a hanging, it is possible to determine if it was suicide or homicide by the position of the pupils. In the case of suicide, the pupils will roll up, whereas in a homicide, the pupils will roll down. If the mucus from the hanging victims nose is a regular colour there is a possibility of revival.

"Ekkinkyo"

(5) If the cause of death is poison the body will appear swollen. There is a good chance of recovery in most cases of poisoning.

(6) Attempt to bend the fingers or toes of the body to determine if Kappo will be helpful. If they can be bent, there is an opportunity to administer Kappo.

(Author's note: In the interest of clarity and brevity, some Kappo revival techniques have been abbreviated, edited or left out altogether.)

Once patients have been revived, it is advisable to lie them on their back and allow them to rest. They will need fresh air, so arrange adequate ventilation. If their recovery appears slow, you may have to cool their head and warm their feet. In some cases, a little alcohol can prove beneficial. If the body is tembling however, alcohol is not recommended. In these cases, a stimulant is required.

To wake the person, pat their face gently and softly call their name. Never throw water on the victim as the shock may cause the opposite effect of that which you require. If the body is trembling and the person is unconscious their breathing will become laboured and the colour will drain from their face. Additionally, the fingernails and lips will become purple. This is a very serious situation which requires immediate medical attention.

It must be remembered that the techniques of Kappo were the result of trial and error. At present, modern medical science has made such advances that if a doctor is available, and the situation merits it, you must judge what will be the better treatment for the victim; to use Kappo, or to rush them to the hospital.

Prevention and Treatment of Karate Injuries Using Kappo

Head injuries. The most common head injury is a concussion, which results in loss of consciousness for a short period. A blow to the chin and falls are the usual way this condition occurs. A concussion rarely results in a loss of consciousness of more than five minutes. Often, the period of unconsciousness is less than ten seconds. The patient may even be unaware of the injury, as the period of unconsciousness may only be momentary. Loss of consciousness is caused by lack of oxygen resulting from shrinkage of the blood vessels. Instances of brief loss of consciousness, followed by clarity, with an ensuing deep unconsciousness, are extremely serious. Equally dangerous are many of the following symptoms, headaches, vomiting, trembling or difficulty in breathing. In any of these cases, the results could be fatal and medical attention should be provided as quickly as possible. All these symptoms indicate the likelihood of damage to the brain and should be treated seriously.

Symptoms may appear at any time during the twenty-four hours following the injury. Therefore, the patient must be observed closely and should rest quietly for two or three days. First aid procedures to treat blows to the head consist of loosening tight clothing (the Karateka's belt), and gently lying the patient on their stomach or side to allow them to breathe freely. If there is a lot of blood as a result of the injury, clean gauze should be applied to the wound. The patient should not be moved unless it is impossible for medical professionals to come to their aid.

Neck injuries. Dislocation and breaking of the neck are of the utmost seriousness. In the case of a dislocation, damage to the spine may result in a restriction of airflow. This will induce paralysis and within a few days, the patient will likely die. In cases where death does not occur, there is a strong possibility of permanent paralysis.

To begin treatment for dislocation, do not move the patient until the neck is stabilized. They should then be transported to hospital as quickly as possible. Today, medical science is extremely advanced compared to the times when knowledge of Kappo was the best care available. There is now doubt as to the effectiveness of the techniques of Kappo. It should be understood, however that the author recommends the use of modern methods of medical attention in the case of serious injury to ensure the safety of the patient.

The following eight Kappo techniques and their application are detailed in Section 2 of the Training Guide: Jokatsu Kokyuho, Haikatsu Yudoho, Kin Kappatsu Shinpo, Haikatsu Kyukiho, Sokatsu Kikaiho, Kokatsu Kashoho, Suikatsu Tosuiho and Sokatsu Seigyoho.

Chinese Kempo and Ti

In comparing Ti and Chinese Kenpo, one finds many common principles. For example, both use the entire body as defensive and offensive weapons. There is, however, a fundamental difference in emphasis that gives Ti its essential character. Chinese Kenpo utilizes techniques that principally employ the open hand or fingertips (shi to). Conversely, Ti relies primarily on the bones of the fist (ken Kotsu). Some Kenpo training points for consideration are included in Section 3 of the Training Guide.

In the Ryukyus, martial arts practitioners have long used natural objects, such as trees and rocks to condition their bodies. An example may be found in their use of the machiwara (Japanese - makiwara). Originally, machi-wara were trees encircled with rice-stalk rope that were struck by practitioners.

More modern versions include a plank of wood wrapped with rope and inserted into the ground. The first written historical reference to this training apparatus appeared in 1850 in an article by Nagoshi Sagenta in the Nanto Zatsua (Southern island culture) broadsheet. In this book *Okinawa no Karate Do*, Funakoshi Gichin describes the machiwara and its application in martial arts training. It was his position that it was uniquely Okinawan, bearing no traces of Chinese Kenpo.

It is widely accepted that Chinese Kenpo was a major source of influence on the development of Ti. One should also remember that given Okinawa's geographical position, the islands have also been exposed to other South Asian cultures. This archipelago, located off the coasts of China and mainland Japan, lies the East China Sea and Pacific Ocean. As a result, Okinawa has become a melting pot for many varied cultural elements. The result is a unique heritage that equals, or surpasses its sources.

Training with the machiwara.

Theories as to how these external influences came to Okinawa are generally based more on conjecture than historical fact. It should be noted, however, that an ancient log of shipwrecks, Ryukyu Hoyoryu Ki, includes a record of a Chinese vessel washed ashore in the fifteenth century. The ship's crew spent considerable time on Okinawa where they taught martial arts to the native population.

Additionally, Chinese records document interaction between people from the Ryukyus and Malaysia in the 1300's. The Ryukyu islands were a convenient stop-over for traders between China and Japan. There are also numerous accounts of Kyukyuans travelling to China to study Kenpo and returning to their homeland to teach. It has been suggested that professional exponents of martial arts travelled considerably and through these experts, Kenpo was likely transmitted.

The forms Wansu and Kusanku are believed to have been introduced in this manner. Further for hundreds of years, beginning in 1392, Sapposhi (Chinese envoys), and their entourage, were invited to the Ryukyus by various kings. They shared many aspects of Chinese culture with local people, including combative methodologies. These events appear to support some of Miyagi Chojun's theories regarding the introduction of Kenpo to Okinawa, as outlined in his book *Ryukyu Kenpo Do Enkaku Gaiyo*. This famed Karateka believed that the unique fighting art of 'To di' originated in Shina (or Ch'ing[5]), China, primarily from two styles of Kenpo; 'Naika' and 'Saika.'

Naika Kenpo, practiced outside the Shaolin monastery, served as the foundation for Buto (Japanese) or Wudong (Chinese) Kenpo. 'Wudong' refers to a school of martial arts originating in the Wudong Mountains. Saika Kenpo, practiced inside the Shaolin monastery, had a profound effect on the development of Shaolin Kenpo.

King Sho Hashi.

---

[5] 'Shina' or 'Ch'ing' may refer to a place (in China) or period of rule, or to the actual rulers themselves.

Weapons Prohibition Laws

Okinawan history is filled with myths, legends and folklore that provide insight into the evolution of this culturally rich area. One example is the annual 'Tsuna Hiki' celebration.

Every October during the festival of the Ryukyus, thousands of visitors to Okinawa witness the world's largest tug-of-war (tsuna hiki). This event is a symbolic re-enactment of the struggle between Gosamaru and Amawari that took place during the reign of King Sho Taikyu (1454-1460).

The annual Tsuna Hiki celebration.

The King feared the powerful armies of Gosamaru and Amawari, two neighbouring 'anji' or 'aji' (chieftain warriors) who had become wealthy through foreign trade. In an effort to thwart any alliance between these two chiefs and to strengthen his own political position, King Sho Taikyu arranged for his daughter, Momoto Fumiagari to marry Amawari. In a battle in 1458, Amawari killed Gosamaru. King Sho Taikyu retained power, until he was succeeded by his son.

As a result of these types of civil conflicts that occurred during various times in Ryukyuan history, there were laws instituted forbidding anyone other than the ruling classes to own weapons.

An example of one such weapons edict was enacted during the reign of King Sho Shin (1477-1526). In an effort to control insurrection by local noblemen, the King issued a royal decree banning private ownership of swords and other fighting implements. Additionally, he demanded lords abandon their fortresses and reside in his castle district in Shuri. It is believed that these periods of disarmament fostered the development of 'empty hand' self defense, or Okinawan Ti.

The use of traditional tools, such as the bo (staff), eku or kai (oak), kama (sickle), nunchaku (flail), and tuifa (handle) also developed any real opposition to the rulers - a civilian population armed with sticks would stand no chance against trained soldiers using steel bladed weapons. In an individual confrontation however, armed with the element of surprise, a skilled martial artist might have a fighting chance.

The abduction of Princess Momoto Fumiagari.

A more striking example of the results of superior weaponry was apparent with the Satsuma invasion of the Ryukyus in 1609. This aggressive action, known as 'Keicho no Eki' lasted only two weeks because the invading forces were armed with firearms. The Okinawans had no experience with guns and were quickly defeated. The invading army reinforced the weapons prohibition policy which would remain in effect for nearly three hundred years. Ryukyuans did not produce iron and instead, crafted farm tools from wood. When iron was used, for example, by government appointed blacksmiths, or in some cases, in producing cooking utensils or agricultural implements, it had to be imported. Its distribution was strictly regulated. As a result of limited access to this valuable metal, firearms were not available to the general population in Okinawa, giving way for the martial arts to flourish.

Ryukyuan Life in the 19th Century

As previously noted, there is little, or no, written documentation of Karate by the masters who developed and preserved 'To di.' We do find, however, detailed references regarding Ryukyuan daily life in the 19th century in the book *Dai Ryukyu to Kokaiki* (Chronicles of the Great Loo Choo) by the English author Basil C. Hall. The book is a geographical and cultural study of the Ryukyuan islands. It was recorded by Westerners during a forty day visit in 1816.

In addition to documenting the practice of Karate, Hall also described many aspects of indigenous culture. These included native construction methods, traditional clothing and dance styles. Hall characterised the Ryukyuans as kind, polite and friendly. He deduced that they

ere philosophically and physically opposed to war based on the fact that the locals had no
eapons. While his observations concerning the gentle disposition of the Ryukyuan people
ppeared to be correct, the true reason for their lack of arms was the enactment of various
eapons prohibition laws.

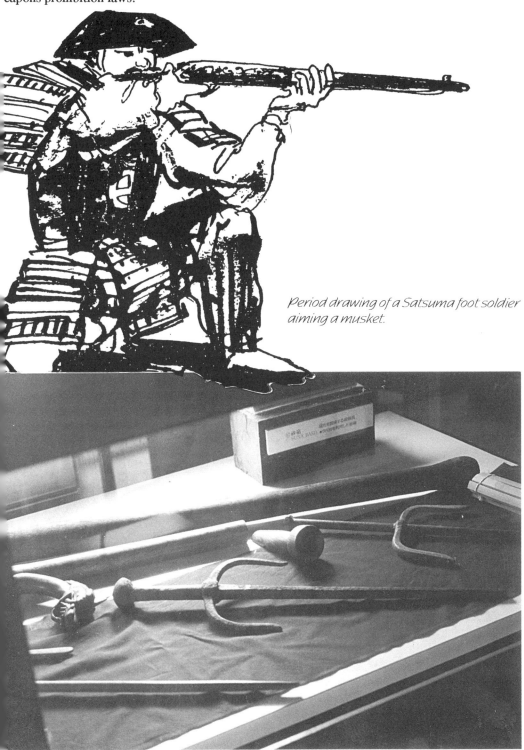

Period drawing of a Satsuma foot soldier aiming a musket.

Traditional weapons.

The book *Chuzan Heishi Riyaku* (Daily Life in the Shuri Castle Area) published in 1832, examines Ryukyuan culture of the period. It features a detailed map, indicating the location of towns and villages. It also includes descriptions of traditional clothing and a catalogue of musical instruments. The book contains a discussion of Okinawan Kenpo and other martial techniques such as horse riding and archery. Mention is also made of the knowledge of firearms, although the availability of such weapons was severely restricted. *Chuzan Heishi Riyaku* also offers interesting martial advice, including "..... an enemy encountered to the front should be felled with the fist, while an enemy to the rear should be felled with the foot."

Another book documenting Ryukyuan customs which mentions martial arts, is *Oshima Hikki*, published in 1762. Additional references may be found in the 1850 publication *Nanto Zatsuwa*.

Oshima Hikki describes a journey undertaken in 1762 by a group of Okinawans who embarked on a trip to Satsuma, now the Japanese prefecture of Kagoshima. Strong winds and adverse weather conditions forced the ship off-course. The travelers landed and took shelter in Tosa, Oshima. During their stay in Tosa, they were interviewed by the book's author Mr. Tobe. They

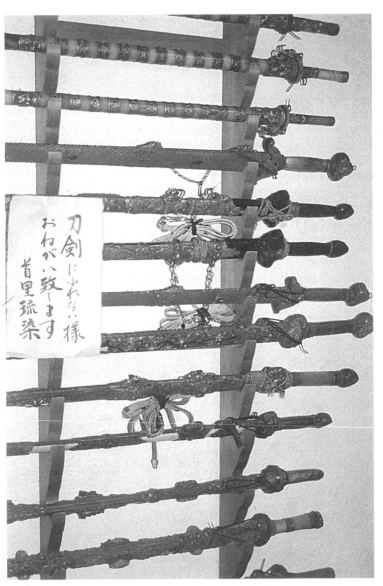

Collection of unique Okinawan swords.

discussed the introduction of Kenpo to the Ryukyus by a "Chinese person" (believed to be the envoy Kushanku). This is a significant event in martial arts history. Until this time, no mention has ever been made, in writing, of 'To di.' To di, or Kenpo, is described in this book as a new 'technique of combination' which utilized punching, kicking and grappling. This bears some similarity to the modern day Goju-ryu practice of 'Kakie,' which features grabbing, pushing and seizing.

Mr. Taira (L) & Mr. Shinzato (R) engage in single-hand "kakie" practice.

Commodore Perry enters Shuri castle through the Shuri mon gate.

27

"Hard" "Soft"

*The author (L) and Mr. Kawasumi (R)
demonstrate a double-hand "kakie" drill.*

The Influence of other Ancient Art Forms

In addition to the influence of several styles, other, non-martial arts are believed to have fuelled the evolution of Karate and Kobudo.

An interesting note concerning this assimilation process is that elements of a style of ancient native Okinawan dance 'mekata' (literally, 'way of dancing') and specifically, a dance form known as 'ti mai,' were integrated into this hybrid system.

Many Okinawan martial arts masters have studied traditional dance forms with the dual purpose of more fully understanding the sources of Ti and of preserving their culture. Visitors to Okinawa are often intrigued by the fact that most Ryukyuans sing, dance, or play an instrument it is a natural part of their rich cultural heritage. Historically, dance, music and other arts have played an important role in the development of many types of martial systems.

Mr. Shiroma demonstrates a classical "Ti" posture.

29

Okinawan folk-dancer. Note the similarity to "Ti" posture.

The Bubishi and its Influence on Okinawan Martial Arts

Often dubbed the 'bible' or 'encyclopedia' of martial arts, the Bubishi is a book of tremendous significance for all practitioners, regardless of style or discipline.

Its thirty-two chapters contain detailed knowledge regarding the mechanics and internal chemistry of the human body. This information can be used to heal or harm. The vital points of the body are clearly defined and the function of each of these points is meticulously explained. This mysterious book was read in very select circles. If a practitioner was deemed worthy of being entrusted with this powerful information, their teacher would permit them to copy one page at a time.

Arrival of the Bubishi in Okinawa

How the Bubishi came to Okinawa is a question with many different answers. There are reliable reports of the book's existence in Okinawa one hundred years ago. Conversely, some experts claim it came to the island more than two hundred years ago, with travelers who risked their lives crossing the tempestuous see between the Ryukyus and China. The most widely accepted theory proposes that Higaonna Kanryo traveled to Fuchou in the 1870's where he copied his teacher's, Kojo Taitei's, text. Higaonna also studied with the legendary Ru Ru Ko and Wai Xinxian. They too, may have supplied him with the Bubishi.

Okinawans hold all things Chinese in high esteem. There are several historical references in a variety of books to thiry-six families. These groups represented numerous industries and interests - from construction and shipbuilding, to a broad range of cultural pursuits.

Beginning in 1393, and for the next five hundred years, these experts would journey to Kume village in Okinawa. There, they established Chinese rule and spread their culture among the local people. Some practitioners hold the belief that the Bubishi was brought to Okinawa by one of these cultural missions, but factual reports are inconclusive.

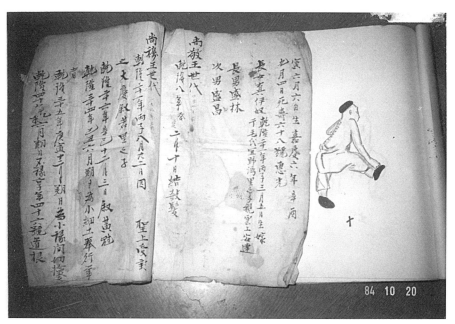

Photograph of a page from the legendary "martial bible", the "Bubishi".

Martial deity from the "Bubishi".

"Bubishi"

The following is an excerpt from the Bubishi.

If you know the enemy well enough and you also know yourself,
then you can gain victory.
If you know yourself well, but you do not know the enemy,
you have an even chance of victory.
If you know neither the enemy nor yourself,
then you will lose the contest without question.

If you have to fight, observe your enemy's weakness and
be sure to use them to your advantage. Fight only if you have assessed the situation and
are assured of victory. Injury is to be avoided at all costs.
Train the body and mind a great deal to limit the risk of being injured.

You are to attack when your opponent is excited or anxious.
You can read their inner state through their eyes.
This is vitally important.

If an opponent holds you from behind,
you must reverse the position to effect your attack.

If your arm is pulled from behind, attack the opponent's face.

If your opponent bites you, attack their throat which will force them to release their bite.

When fighting an opponent,
the most important consideration is the distance between the two of you.
Control this distance and you control the fight.

Maintain your balance at all times, especially when you make your attack.
A loss of balance provides an opportunity for a counter-attack.

If the opponent grabs your clothing and you are pulled close to them,
use your knees as weapons to strike and injure him.
If you cause enough pain, he will release his grip immediately.

Kenpo training emphasizes the development of balanced breathing.
Remember this training in combat.

Never relax your guard until victory is assured.
Even if you knock your opponent down,
you must then subdue him as quickly as possible.
Do not allow a moment of respite for him, or you will risk your life.

If your opponent staggers, be cautious as he may try to attack your legs.

An opponent who crouches will not attack with his feet.
You must be prepared for him to attack with his hands.

Beware of employing kicks to your opponent's upper body
as this posture jeopardizes your balance.
Be sure you can retain balance in this situation.

Attack your opponent with your hands first.
Then step on his feet to immobilize and overbalance him.

If your opponent takes hold of your sleeve,
you can counter with a thrust of your fingertips to an appropriate vital point.

"Tatsujin = Meigin"

PART TWO
Martial Arts Pioneers

Sakugawa Kanga. Born in 1735, Sakugawa Kanga is the first Okinawan to be credited with the development of 'To di.' As previously noted, these combative systems were amalgamations of traditional Okinawan 'Ti' and Chinese Kenpo. More than two hundred years ago, Sakugawa spent considerable time in China immersed in an advanced study of martial arts. He then introduced Kenpo to the Ryukyus. Upon his return to Okinawa, he taught 'To di,' the name used to describe combative arts, until the end of the 1800's. In recognition of his significant contribution to their culture, the Okinawan people dubbed him 'Todi Sakugawa.'

Stored in the personal library of Higaonna Sensei is a magnificent detailed map dating from the year 1700. Covering the space of six tatami mats, it is larger than the size of a small, modern Tokyo apartment. It features a wealth of interesting historical information including drawings of Ryukyuan cities, as well as the precise location of the home of 'Todi Sakugawa.' Clearly, this notation stands as further testimony to Sakugawa's role as an important historical figure among the Ryukyuan people.

Matsumura Sokon. Reports as to the actual birthdate of 'Bushi' Matsumura vary - from 1796 to 1799 or 1809. During a life that spanned more than ninety years, this martial arts legend played a key role in the development of Okinawan Budo. Matsumura was a student of Sakugawa Kanga and the famous Chinese instructor Kong Shu Kung ('Kushanku'). He served as bodyguard for the Ryukyuan Kings Sho Ko, Sho Iku and Sho Tai. This occupation provided ample opportunity for travel to Duchou, Chine, where he trained with Iwah and Ason. He also journeyed to Satsuma, on the mainland, where he studied the clan's combative style of Jigen-ryu. His student roster reads like a who's who of Okinawan martial arts and includes, Itosu Anko, Kuwae Ryusei, Yabu Kensetsu, Hanashiro Chomo, Funakoshi Gichin and Kyan Chotoku.

The burial site and monument to Matsumura Sokon in Tomari.
His birthplace is nearby.

Sadly, despite Matsumura's pursuit of martial excellence and his impressive teaching credentials, he is most often remembered for subduing a tethered bull. Reportedly, he struck the animal repeatedly with a stick for more than a week. Later, in a public demonstration designed to showcast 'Bushi's' martial prowess, the frightened beast ran from Matsumura. Rather than dwell on this less than impressive feat, martial artists should recall Matsumura's combative skill, his talent as a calligrapher and his scholarly studies of the Chinese classics. These demonstrate his belief that balance between physical accomplishments and confucian knowledge will result in peace and harmony.

Higaonna Kanryo. 'Higashionna,' or as he would later be known, Higaonna, was born in 1853 in the west section of Naha. A child of a poor family of shizoku class, young Kanryo's academic education was cut short as he was compelled to seek out employment. To earn a meager living, he performed a variety of menial jobs such as porter, night watchman, boat hand and firewood gatherer.

His martial arts education reportedly began when he was a teenager. He studied with the noted To di teacher Arakaki Seisho of Kume mura. Arakaki was scheduled

to travel to Peking for an undetermined stay. In order to ensure Higaonna could continue his martial arts study uninterrupted, Arakaki introduced him to Kojo Taitei. A benevolent benefactor, the wealthy Kojo financed Higaonna's travel to Fuchou in 1873. He remained there for approximately ten years, training with Kojo in his Chinese dojo. He also studied with other teachers, including Wan Shien Ling, commonly referred to as Ru Ru Ko. Wan Shien Ling was a shoemaker by profession, but his passion was Chinese boxing. Although the two men were close in age, Higaonna referred to Wan Shien Ling as 'older brother' or 'old man,' evidence of the affection and respect he had for his instructor.

Although Kiyoda Juhatsu classified Higaonna's style as Hsing-I boxing, he, in fact, studied White Crane. Additionally, contrary to descriptions of modern Goju practitioners, he is remembered by many of his contemporaries as being 'quick' and 'lightfooted.'

When Higaonna Sensei died in 1916, at the age of 63, he named Miyagi Chojun as his successor.

1936 meeting of the most influential Okinawan teachers of the period, sponsored by the Showa Kaikan. Front row, left to right: Chotoku Kyan, Kentsu Yabu, Chomo Hanashiro, Chojun Miyagi. Back row, left to right: Shinpan Shiroma, Tsuyoshi Chitose, Chosin Chibana and Kenwa Nakasone.

Rare photograph of an early Goju-ryu training practice.
Miyagi Chojun is centre at the rear. Also pictured
are Madan Bashi Keiyo, Higa Seikou and Shinzato Jinan.

Gathering of Karate masters and local dignitaries
at the 1992 re-opening of Shuri Castle.
From left to right: Shugara Nakazato, Katsuya Miyahira, Seikichi Uehara,
Meitoku Yagi, Shoshin Nagamine and Ychoku Higa.

Miyagi Chojun.   Miyagi Sensei was born April 25, 1888 and died on October 8, 1953. Twenty-five years after his death, his noteworthy contributions to Japanese Karate were celebrated during a memorial ceremony at the Meiji shrine.

When Miyagi Sensei was a young man of sixteen, he traveled to Fukkensho (Fuchou), China, where he studied Kenpo. When he returned to Okinawa, he brought with him a book entitled Bubishi. It contained detailed knowledge and numerous secrets about martial arts training. With the aid of this invaluable document, Miyagi founded his own style of Karate - Goju-ryu.

At age thirty-nine, Miyagi received a teaching appointment in Japan at the Ritsumeikan University in Kyoto.

Miyagi Sensei was one of the most influential Okinawans to teach in mainland Japan, leaving a strong organisation that flourishes to the present. The goal of his teaching and research, was to pass his knowledge on to his students in order that karate would develop more rapidly. There can be no doubt that Miyagi Sensei achieved this noble aim.

Miyagi Chojun with students.

Miyagi Chojun.

39

Miyagi Chojun (far left) observes class.

Left to right: Miyagi Chojun with his top students - Meitoku Yagi, Eichi Miyazato, Seikichi Toguchi, and Eiko Miyazato.

Miyagi Chojun in 1935. To his left is Mr. Nakamoto.
Seated in front of Miyagi Sensei is Mr. Shiroma
and to his right is Mr. Azama.

Funakoshi Gichin. Often called 'the father of modern karate' Funakoshi Gichin, founder of Shotokan Karate-do, studied with Itosu Anko, Asato Anko and Matsumura Sokon.

Itosu Sensei recognised that martial arts were extremely beneficial in building a strong body and a disciplined mind. He advocated the introduction of Karate as a compulsory subject in Okinawan junior high schools during the Meiji period 34-35. School authorities saw this as an opportunity to improve the overall quality of their education system.

Funakoshi shared Itosu's vision and believed that Karate philosophy would enlighten young minds. He encouraged practitioners to develop a heart so full of truth that greed and evil thoughts would be prevented from entering. Funakoshi Sensei and other instructors believed this ideal is also valid from a physical standpoint. If your body is strong, an enemy will be less inclined to attack you. If you encounter another traveler on your path and you give way for him to pass, there will be no conflict. If neither person yields however, the stand-off will inevitably lead to an altercation. Conflict in this instance, is a result of stubbornness, a vice which often leads to war. Karate teaches us to resolve conflict and to share with others.

The weak are to be protected and the evil are to be subdued. This is achieved not through direct confrontation, but rather, through an impenetrable defense.

Funakoshi Sensei portrays Karate as a graceful and gentle art with a strong cultural tradition. This makes it most appealing to the human spirit. Through diligent study and practice that can be performed anywhere, techniques can be memorized. Correct, regular training can result in improved health and vitality.

Karate, a unique form of personal defense, is different from other martial arts. Well-conditioned hands and feet are its primary weapons. Both the hands and the feet are used equally in Karate. The result is a formidable fighting system. In Funakoshi's opinion, of all the martial arts, it is Karate that is best suited to women seeking an efficient method of self-defense.

Most classical martial arts, such as Karate, Judo, Sumo, Aikido and Kendo, require you to train in your bare feet. On the soles of the feet there is a point called 'yusen.' Stimulating this area can be good for the heart and kidneys. Karate training combines stimulation of the 'yusen' point with breathing techniques that invigorate the entire body and improve circulation. It is not surprising then, that when asked how to ensure a long, healthy life, Okinawans advise vigorous Karate training.

Funakoshi's Karate teachers are prime examples of the physical, mental and spiritual benefits of martial training. They were productive, healthy and lived into their eighties. Having trained since childhood, they credited Karate for their longevity and vitality.

*Extremely rare photograph of Funakoshi
Gichin engaged in bo-sai kumite.*

Mabuni Kenwa. The founder of Shito-ryu, Mabuni Sensei was born in the year 1889 and began his Karate education at an early age. He was not a very robust child and his parents decided that martial arts training could improve his health. Mabuni proved to be a conscientious student and his strength and health improved immensely.

As an adult, Mabuni began teaching Karate to students in local high schools, as well as to the Okinawan police force. He later moved to Osaka in mainland Japan where he opened a dojo.

Mabuni Sensei was avidly interested in a variety of martial arts and other sports and he applied their principles to his Karate teaching. A true innovator, Mabuni Sensei developed protectors for Karate by studying equipment used for Kendo, boxing and baseball.

As with other great teachers, Mabuni Sensei was zealous in promoting Karate. He was a prolific writer and authored many books about the martial arts. Further, he formed 'Kenyoukai,' a study group established to research Karate's history and technical development.

Mabuni Kenwa (centre), Junakoshi Gichin (far left) and students.

Mabuni Kenwa performing movements from Pinan kata.

Kiyoda Juhatsu. Kiyoda Juhatsu was born in Naha in 1886 and died in the mainland in 1968. His martial arts education began at age thirteen. Although he started training only a short while before Miyagi, the latter referred to him as 'senpai.'

His style, Toon-ryu, was named after his instructor Higaonna, using the first two kanji characters of his revered teacher's name. It is characterised by quick, 'springing' movements, which place little emphasis on rooted stances. Additionally, Toon-ryu relies on the use of kicks to low targets.

Higaonna also instructed Kiyoda Sensei in the use of Chinese weapons. Kiyoda rounded-out his education by studying White Crane Boxing with Go Kenki. Consequently, the Toon-ryu rendition of Nepai closely resembles the Chinese version.

Kiyoda Sensei played an instrumental role in supporting Higaonna's efforts to introduce Karatedo into the Naha Shiritsu Shogyo School. As a high school teacher, he was well suited to instructing students in the martial arts. He achieved a fair degree of prominence in this area. Later, upon retiring from his teaching post, he became a professional Karate Sensei, first in Okinawa and then in southern Japan.

His friends and colleagues included Mabuni Kenwa, Taira Shinken, Toyama Kanken, Konishi Yasuhiro and Chitose Tsuyoshi.

In 1934, the Dai Nippon Butokukai named him director and head instructor for the Naha, Okinawan branch. Three years later, he received a special merit award from the Butokukai (Kyoto).

Kiyoda Sensei helped popularize mainland budo customs. These included the use of the teaching titles Shihan, Renshi, Kyoshi and Hanshi.

Kiyoda Juhatsu.

Kiyoda Juhatsu in traditional dress.

Kiyoda Juhatsu is also remembered for the respect and humility he demonstrated at the end of each class. After training, he would speak at length and with considerable reverence, acknowledging his teacher Higaonna Sensei.

Kiyoda Juhatsu (R) practicing kumite with Miyagi Chojun(L).

Nakasone Seiyu. Nakasone Sensei was born in Naha-shi on January 15, 1893. His Karate training began at age twelve and continued until his death on April 20, 1983. When his teachers, Koutatsu Iha, Matsumura Kosaku, Yoshihito Maeda and Nakazato died, he was the logical heir to the Tomari (Tumai di) legacy. It wasn't until the end of World War 2, however, that he actually opened his own dojo.

Although reports about Nakasone Sensei's colourful youth (e.g. tales of goat striking and beer bottle 'chopping') are widespread, he was a deeply philosophical person. He taught his disciples that the aim of Karate is to create a sense of peace in society. This is achieved by individuals taking responsibility for the care of their family and partners. Futhermore, one must maintain an attitude of politeness when dealing with all people. Sincerity, love and courage are the philosophies we should live by, was what Nakasone Sensei believed, as well as, that if you are polite and self-disciplined you will commit no transgressions.

Nakasone Seiyu poses beside a photograph of himself as a young man.

Higga Seiko. Higa Seiko was born in Naha-shi Okinawa on November 8, 1898. He began his martial arts training at age 13, under the famed instructor Higaonna. Following his teacher's death, he continued his studies with Miyagi Chojun, founder of Goju-ryu. Higa Sensei was a well-educated man who was employed as an elementary school teacher. Later, he began a lengthy career as a policeman. Finally, he followed the path of a Karate Sensei. He dedicated his life to bringing the martial arts and their benefits to young people.

Higa Sensei first taught Karate on the island of Saipan located in the South Pacific, where he lived for two years. On his return to Okinawa, the title of Shihan (Master) was bestowed upon him by Miyagi Chojun. He received this honour in recognition of his excellence and devotion in teaching Karate. This was an historic event as it was the only time Miyagi awarded a teaching certificate. Higa Sensei continued to teach Karate for many years. He instructed students in his dojo, a local high school, and the University of the Ryukyus.

During his summer holidays, he also taught martial arts to the wardens and guards of the Okinawan prison. A man of few words, his succinct motto was - peace. He believed that even though styles differ, Karate's essence is one, everyone must strive to help one another and work to better the world.

I was fortunate to have studied with Higa Seiko. Many memories come to mind as I picture him in the dojo wearing his traditional red belt. His school was very popular and classes were always crowded with zealous Karateka. On occasion, American karate students visited. It was in this dojo, that I learned the correct way to block and counter. Additionally, I can vividly recall lessons on the machiwara. Higa Sensei taught me the importance of using hip rotation and muscle contraction to generate power. He also emphasized the significance of controlling one's breath when engaged in machiwara practice. In many Karate dojos throughout the world, there are versions of the machiwara. With each strike of the devout practitioner, one hears an audible testament to the great heritage of ancient Okinawan martial arts.

In May 1956 meeting at the dojo of Nagamine Shoshin, nineteen Karate teachers assembled to establish the Okinawan Ken Karate-do Renmei (First All Okinawan District Association). Higa Sensei was elected vice-chairman on this day and four years later became the organisation's chairman. Higa Sensei believed that the true purpose of Karate was to serve the public and promote friendship throughout the world. In keeping with this philosophy, he broadened the scope of this association and renamed it Koskusai Karate Kobudo Renmei (International Karate Kobudo League).

On April 16, 1966, Higa Seikou died at the age of 68. He is survived by many disciples who continue to espouse the traditions of Okinawan Karate-do, among them his son Higa Seikichi. His mission is to uphold his family's tradition of promoting Karate worldwide.

Higa Seiko (L) with Taira Shinken (R).

Higa Seiko performing a posture from the "Bubishi."

Higa Seiko (L) and Fukuchi Seiko (R) Izumigawa Kanki (centre).

Rare photo of Higa Seikou with his class.

*Sanchin training
at the Higa dojo.*

Fukuchi Seiko. Fukuchi Sensei was born in Naha-shi, Okinawa on August 4th during the eighth year of the Taisho period. While in junior high school, he began studying Karate with Higa Sensei. He eventually became a teacher at the Hombu dojo where I studied under his expert guidance.

Although he died at the early age of 56 on July 8th, Showa 50 period, Fukuchi Sensei became an important figure in the world of Okinawan Karate.

Fukuchi Seiko.

Fukuchi Seiko posing with tuifa.

The following is a transcript of a discussion held in 1958 between five Karateka who traveled to Japan with Fukuchi Sensei as their spokesman. Their purpose was to promote Okinawan Karate through demonstration and discussion.

Morikawa: *(3rd Dan Goju-ryu) (moderator): I suggest that all martial arts were influenced by the place in which they were practiced. Consequently, they developed individual characteristics in spite of common origins. Examine the differences between Chinese Kenpo and Japanese Karate - even though they both originated in China.*

Fukuchi Sensei, you practice Okinawan Goju-ryu which I believe is different from Japanese Goju-ryu, isn't it?

Fukuchi: (8th Dan Goju-ryu): Yes, that's true. Japanese Karate has evolved its own way since its original introduction to the mainland. The fact that communication between Okinawa and Japan was restricted after the war made it necessary for the Japanese to develop their own methods of teaching Karate.

Morikawa: *Were you a disciple of Miyagi Sensei?*

Fukuchi: No. Miyagi Sensei taught my teacher, Higa Sensei.

Morikawa: *When did you join Higa Sensei's dojo?*

Fukuchi: When I was 13 years old. I was not very strong so I began training to fortify my body.

Morikawa: *Was the training at the dojo particularly strenuous?*

Fukuchi: Yes, it was very hard. Each kata took a year to master. I had to perform the fundamental breathing kata, Sanchin, every day, over and over, until I was exhausted. I remember being so tired that I couldn't stand up to go to the bathroom! Most students quit after three months.

Morikawa: *The training is still essentially the same. If students can get through the first six months, they can train for years. This has always been the way for Karate training, but I think that perhaps it was more difficult in Fukuchi Sensei's day then it is now.*

Fukuchi: Perhaps, but I also heard it said that it was far tougher in the days before I began training.

Morikawa: *Miyagi Sensei recalled their rigorous training - especially, the method of breathing. On a stormy day, he would stand at the edge of a cliff and practice Sanchin to ensure correct technique and full concentration. If he had made a mistake in his breathing, he would fall to his death.*

Fukuchi: Miyagi Sensei was a very severe person. In contrast, Higa Sensei appeared mild.

Morikawa: *By the way, is it true that you are a 3rd Dan in Kendo?*

Fukuchi: Yes. I have always encouraged my students to study Kendo or other martial arts. I find there is much in common between Kendo and Karate.

Iha: (4th Dan Goju-ryu): I agree. For example, footwork and body positioning are similar in both disciplines.

Fukuchi: Okinawan dance is also the same.

Morikawa: *I notice you all have exceptionally strong hands. I've heard that long ago, people would strike their hands with a hammer to destroy the nerves in an effort to desensitize themselves. Do you train in this way?*

Taba: (4th Dan Goju-ryu): No. We perform basics correctly every day using the machiwara. This makes our hands very strong. To break anything with your hands, however, you also need to have a powerful wrist. Unless you train to strengthen both the fist and wrist, your training will be meaningless.

Kishaba: (4th Dan Goju-ryu): First, we have to train the feet and legs. I jog two kilometers every morning to condition my feet and legs and develop stamina. There should be no rest periods during training. It should be continuous and intense.

Morikawa: Fukuchi Sensei, I understand that your school has its own method of training.

Fukuchi: The most important point is to learn the kata thoroughly and to practice them over and over again. In my school, we also use some special tools to enhance our training. For example, we use two heavy jars full of sand called kami. You grasp the jars tightly and travel the length of the dojo in Sanchin stance. This conditions the entire body through strength and breathing drills and also produces a vice-like grip.

Morikawa: What about sai and tuifa?

Taba: These are not Karate weapons. They are used to practice Kobudo in Okinawa, but they can be useful in Karate training. I practice with nunchaku, which are very effective.

*Memorial celebration for Higa Seiko
marking the first anniversary of his death.*

Morikawa: These weapons are made in different sizes according to the size of the student, aren't they?

Iha: Yes. As a general rule, they should be a little longer than your forearm.

Morikawa: Do the same specifications hold true for the sai?

Iha: Yes, the sai and the jutte are closely related.

Morikawa: Is the jutte also made in different sizes?

Kishaba: Yes. I prefer to use weapons that are a little thinner and lighter than customary. Weapons should be made to match each person's power and stature.

Taba: The Okinawan people have used ordinary implements in their training for a very long time. This is one of the ways they have developed their own martial ways.

Morikawa: Are there any other tools of Kobudo that are unique to Okinawa?

Fukuchi: Yes - suruchin, tinbe and eku. There are experts who specialize in each of these weapons. If one trains dilligently, one can achieve Busai.[6]

Morikawa: What is Busai?

Fukuchi: It is best descibed as "martial awareness." For example, in times past, when visiting someone's house, the martial expert would survey the area around the house before entering. Once inside, he would position himself with his back to the wall to prevent an attack from the rear.

Taba: They would sit in a cross-legged position that would enable them to kick in the event of an attack.

Kishaba: There is an old story of a Karate expert who was drinking in a bar one evening with a woman who worked there. A sumo wrestler who was a regular customer, became jealous. He picked the small man up and threw him out of a second storey window. The Karate man lay motionless on the ground. Thinking he had killed him, the sumo wrestler went downstairs to investigate. As soon as the wrestler was close enough, the Karate man threw a powerful kick to his stomach from the ground. The sumo wrestler learned a tough lesson. He died from his injuries.

Morikawa: Wasn't the Karate man hurt at all?

Kishaba: No, he fell to the ground like a cat. Karate practitioners study the movements of animals which can be very helpful in situations such as these.

Fukuchi: If we practice something repeatedly, it eventually becomes natural, reflexive and can then be applied in an emergency.

Iha: I think this is true Budo.

Taba: During a fight, I can predict my opponent's movements by watching his eyes. This enables me to move before he completes his attack. This, too, is Budo.

Kishaba: This reminds me of the Okinawan expression 'kachimira kiri' or 'kachimirari ra kiri' (kick everything if you are attacked). This refers to the method of "catch and kick" taught in To di which recognizes that the kick is the most powerful weapon available.

---

[6] Busai is also described as "martial perfection," a state of combat readiness achieved through constant repetitive practice, wherein martial artists cultivate an intuitive ability to recognize and prevent attacks "before" they occur.

Morikawa: *Why has Karate continued to flourish in Okinawa?*

Taba: Okinawan children grow up with Karate around them, it is part of their cultural heritage, an integral part of their lives. Japanese children do not have this.

Iha: One of the Karate games we played as children was 'gita mun rou' where students hop around on one foot while trying to push the other players over. It made training fun and helped us improve our balance.

Kishaba: When we fight in Okinawa we don't use weapons. It is a question of morality. If adults fight with weapons, they are banished from the region. If children fight with weapons, they will be treated as outcasts. This is the Okinawan way.

Taba: Experts in Karate do not use martial arts if forced to fight an ordinary person. They are aware of the danger of Karate techniques and use them only in a life-threatening encounter.

Fukuchi: In Okinawa, there are many thick stone walls. An enemy could ambush you at any corner. I train my disciples to take a wide angle when turning a corner, staying away from the wall.

Morikawa: *I have also heard that advice. When you approach far from the wall, you can see your enemy and prepare to fight. Fukuchi Sensei, do you have anything to add about Okinawan Karate?*

Fukuchi: Some people think Okinawan Karate is old-fashioned or still practiced in secrecy. The reality is that Japanese Karate has departed from the true styles upon which it was based. Through no fault of Japanese Karateka, this has resulted in a gap that we want to bridge. We want the world to know about true Okinawan Karate.

Kenshikai Seenchin kata.

Taira Shinken. Numerous books published by Taira Sensei's students have lead to widespread awareness of this martial arts expert. He was born in 1897 and died in 1970 and succeeded his teacher Yabiku Moden as head of the Ryukyu Hozon Shinkokai (Promotion and Preservation for Ryukyuan Kobudo). Taira Sensei learned and catalogued approximately thirty bo kata from a variety of sources. Some of these kata were practiced for combative purposes. Others were 'kumi' dances that celebrated cultural, historical and even religious (shamanistic) events. The Kobudo master was also an expert with sai, tuifa, kama, nunchaku, eku, tinbei, tekko and suruchin. He learned, or created, a kata for each weapon. Thanks largely to his efforts, Ryukyu Kobudo became the standard in the mainland for many years.

His two principal students in Okinawa were Nakamoto Masahiro and Akamine Eisuke. Taira Sensei named the latter as his successor. He is also credited with teaching Kobudo to Funakoshi, Konishi, Mabuni, Sakagami, Hayashi and Kokuba. He also instructed Inoue Motokatsu who served as the principle proponent of Okinawan weapons arts in the mainland.

Additionally, this exceptional martial artist was also a Karate expert who trained with Funakoshi and Mabuni. His unique style of Karate, Funakoshi Kempo, is practiced exclusively in the Akamine dojo. This unadulterated form of Karate most closely resembles that which was taught by Funakoshi Gichin.

In these rare photographs, Mabuni Kenwa (R) and Taira Shinken (L) engage in kumite practice.

54

Matayoshi Shinpou. Matayoshi Shinpou was a Karate student of Gokenki (1886-1940). Gokenki, also known as Yoshikawa, was the Chinese Kenpo practitioner credited by many experts with introducing 'Hakutsuru-ken' to the Okinawan martial arts community.

Additionally, Matayoshi Sensei studied Kobudo with his father, Matayoshi Shinko (1888-1947). The elder Matayoshi was a legendary expert. He developed his system of martial arts after traveling to China where he studied Shuriken-jitsu (the art of throwing projectiles) and other forms of weaponry.

Matayoshi Shinpou instructed me in the use of the staff. He admonished me to remember that practice with this simply constructed weapon provides the foundation of Kobudo. As one regards weapons as extensions of the hands and feet, this is a natural outgrowth of Karate training. Practitioners have relied on staffs to extend their reach. Development with respect to the hoe, sword and spear are bases, to a great extent, on the staff.

Matayoshi Sensei had a powerful impact on the preservation and development of traditional martial arts. In addition to teaching, he founded the 'Okinawan Kobudo Renmei,' (Okinawan Ancient Martial Arts Association) in 1970.

American Karate pioneer Anthony Mirakian (far left) and Gory-ryu legend Yagi Meitoku (2nd from right) with their Kobudo teacher Taira Shinken (in black gi).

Portrait of Matayoshi Shinko (from the Matayoshi family collection).

Matayoshi Shinpou (R) with the author (L).

Masters in the Mainland

From the Taisho to the Showa periods (1910-1952), many Okinawan Karate experts taught martial arts to the people of mainland Japan. Among the most notable are some of the legendary instructors previously discussed, as well as others: Funakoshi Gichin, Yabu Kentsu, Miyagi Chojun, Uechi Kanbun, Kiyoda Juhatsu, Shinzato Jinan, Yabiku Mouden, Mabuni Kenwa, Motobu Choki, Shiroma Kouki, Taira Shinken and Chitose Tsuyoshi.

Traditionally, martial arts instruction was limited to a select group, generally through family connections or through closely knit organizations of like-minded individuals. The individual characteristics of each group's method was labeled a 'Ryuha.' Each Ryuha practiced different kata (forms) and bunkai (interpretation of the movements). They employed their own particular methods of training and manner of teaching.

Akamine Eisuke.

"Martial Arts Mind"

Mabuni Kenwa (front row, 2nd from left),
Taira Shinken (3rd from left) and students.

Okinawa Karate do Goju-ryu Association.

沖縄古武道協会(幹部)設立記念　1961.6.17　於7那覇八汐荘

First meeting of the Okinawa Kobudo
Association, held in Naha, June 17, 1961.

第11回全沖縄空手道選手権大会

'88 12 11

11th Okinawa Karate do Championships.

Yabu Kentsu (centre) with his family.

Shiroma Shinpan.

*All Okinawa Karate Kobudo Rengokai
tournament, June 11, 1967.*

第17回

June 25, 1967,
All Okinawa Karate Kobudo meeting.

17th All Okinawa Karate do Association's
Karate and Kobudo Martial Arts tournament,
Heisei 1, October 4th, Senno Bay City Hall.

Yabiku Moden (centre, seated) with
Taira Shinken (pictured with sai).

*Kyan Chotoku (center, seated) with his
students Shiroma Shinpan (right) and Chitose Tsuyoshi (left).*

Master Chitose (L) with his top student Yamamoto Ganyamo.

Demonstration and tournament by the Ryukyu Kobudo Renmei on the 25th anniversary of the death of Matayoshi Shinko.

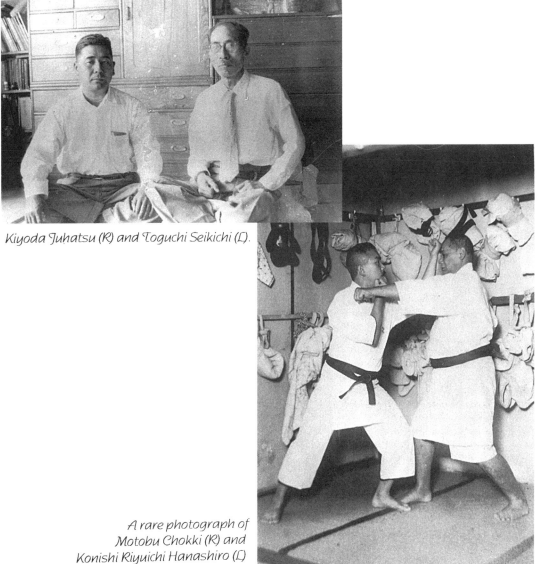

Kiyoda Juhatsu (R) and Toguchi Seikichi (L).

A rare photograph of Motobu Chokki (R) and Konishi Riyuichi Hanashiro (L) sparring.

15th All Okinawa Karate Tournament, Showa 60, September 29,1985, Naha City Arena.

Uechi Kanei (centre, front row) visits Mabuni Kenwa (to his right) with Taira Shinken (front row, right).

1959年6月28日 演武大會並にホワイト君送別記念

*1959 Embutaikan (farewell party) and
tournament in honour of Mr. White.*

"Tomari Ti"   "Naha Ti"   "Sui Ti"

PART THREE
The Evolution of Modern Martial Arts

Shorin and Shorei-ryu

In his book 'Toudi Jikajo,' Itosu Anko states Kenpo has its roots in two styles, Shorin-ryu and Shorei-ryu, both of which came directly from China to Okinawa.

This supposition is corroborated by the Bubishi text and further explored in the writings of Funakoshi Gichin. Funakoshi Sensei describes the differences between the two styles as follows: Shorin-ryu is characterised by speed of movement, whereas Shorei-ryu is distinguished by conditioning through muscle toning exercises. This theory of the origin of the two styles was popularized by Funakoshi and spread throughout mainland Japan. In Okinawa, people refer to the styles originating from Shorin-ryu as 'Shurite' and those from Shorei-ryu as 'Nahate.' This indicates the regions where these styles were embraced and practiced.

In writing his three books, *Ryukyu Kenpo Toudi*, *Goshin Toudi Jutsu* and *Karate Do Kyohan* and in classifying Shorin-ryu and Shorei-ryu kata Funakoshi Gichin developed the chart below.

	A	*B*	*C*
Pinan	*Shorin-ryu 1*	*Shorin-ryu 2*	*Shorin-ryu 2*
Naihanchi	*Shorei-ryu*	*Shorei-ryu*	*Shorei-ryu*
Kosukun	*Shorin-ryu 1*	*Shorin-ryu 2*	*Shorin-ryu 2*
Passai	*Shorin-ryu 1*	*Shorin-ryu 2*	*Shorin-ryu 2*
Seshan	*Shorei-ryu*	*Shorei-ryu*	*Shorei-ryu*
Wanshu	*Shorei-ryu*	*Shorei-ryu*	*Shorin-ryu 2*
Chinto	*Shorei-ryu*	*Shorin-ryu 2*	*Shorin-ryu 2*
Jitte	*Shorei-ryu*	*Shorin-ryu 2*	*Shorei-ryu*
Jion	*Shorei-ryu*	*Shorei-ryu*	*Shorei-ryu*

I am of the opinion that the results of Funakoshi Sensei's research and assignment of these categories are inconsistent. Further, they appear to be in direct opposition to conclusions formulated by other scholars.

Naming Styles

It was not uncommon for early Karateka to honour their instructors' memories, immortalize famous teachers and pay homage to their families when naming their styles. Some examples follow.

Uechi Kanbun - opened a Chinese Kenpo school where he taught a method of To di called 'Panagi-noon.' He later developed a style that would bear his family name - Uechi-ryu.

Miyagi Chojun - developed his style from Naha-te and named it Goju-ryu sourced from the Bubishi.

Funakoshi Gichin - evolved his style from Shurite ('Sui Di' or 'Sui Ti' in the Okinawan 'Hogen' dialect). Much to his chagrin, Master Funakoshi's students would later pay tribute to their instructor and using his pen name 'Shoto,' would christen the style "Shotokan."

Mabuni Kenwa - blended the elements of Sui Di, Tomari Di and Naha Di to formulate Shito-ryu. The name combines the first kanji characters of his teachers' last names Itosu (Shi)

昭林流と昭霊流

"Shorin and Shorei Ryu"

and Higaonna (To).

Kiyoda Juhatsu - called his style Shorei-ryu ("enlightened spirit way") as did his teacher Master Higaonna.

Chibana Chosin "The Last Warrior of Shuri."

The late Higa Yuchko (front row, 3rd from right) and students.

Nakazato Joen.

*Kyan Chotoku (centre, seated) with his
students in front of his dojo in 1941.*

Four Primary Styles

There are four main styles currently practiced in Okinawa which are derived from Shorin-ryu and Shorei-ryu. Shorin-ryu evolved into Shorin-ryu 1 and Shorin-ryu 2. Shorei-ryu was the foundation of Goju-ryu and Uechi-ryu. A list of kata and some specific training methods follows.

Shorin-ryu 1 is the oldest of the four styles. The kata include the following.

(1) Naihanchi 1-3
(2) Pinan 1-5
(3) Passai (dai and sho)
(4) Kusanku (dai and sho)
(5) Chintou
(6) Gojushiho
(7) Jion
(8) Seshan
(9) Unsu
(10) Chintei
(11) Ananku
(12) Wandao
(13) Jitte
(14) Wanshu
(15) Wankuwan
(16) Jiin
(17) Rohai

The basic form, Naihanchi, is practiced by students until the essence of the style is transmitted. The student learns one kata at a time and practices it for a long period before the teacher introduces a new form.

Shorin-ryu 2 while very similar to Shorin-ryu 1, the method of training is different. Tremendous emphasis is placed on calesthenics and repetition of individual techniques. A training outline follows:

- A warm up period of exercising the entire body is essential.
- Fundamental exercises are repeated many times during each training session and can be divided into the following categories: - upper body striking techniques
                                                                   - blocking techniques
                                                                   - kicking techniques
                                                                   - footwork drills

- Aerobic and resistance exercises (e.g. skipping rope and lifting weights) are used to develop speed, strength and stamina.
- Kata and their applications, are practiced repeatedly.
- Kumite drills with a partner are utilized to simulate actual combat situations.
- Machiwara practice is an essential training component.
- Verbal instruction, in the form of lecture, is also employed to ensure students cultivate a deeper understanding of the nuances of this style.

Kata include:

(1) Fukyugata 1
(2) Pinan 1-5
(3) Wankuwan
(4) Rohai
(5) Naihanchi
(6) Passai
(7) Chintou
(8) Kusanku
(9) Gojushiho

Monument honouring Itosu Anko.

Miyahira Katsuya.

Goju-ryu was founded by Higaonna (sometimes written Higashionna) whose chief disciple was Miyagi Sensei. Methods of training advocated in this style include calisthenics to warm up the body and resistance exercises to develop strength.

    (1) Gekisai 1 + 2
    (2) Seyunchin
    (3) Saifa
    (4) Shishochin
    (5) Sanseiru
    (6) Seisan
    (7) Kururunfa
    (8) Sanchin
    (9) Seipai
   (10) Tenshou
   (11) Suparinpei (or Pechurin)

Sanchin kata is the foundation of Goju-ryu. Instructors would require students to practice this form many times during each training session. Additionally, sanchin stance would be practiced by students carrying heavy weights walking the length of the dojo floor. Kumite, as a controlled but spirited form of combat enabled students to improve their reaction speed while under pressure of attack. Analysis and the memorizing of the kata, were clearly, key training elements. Special emphasis was devoted to perfecting each kata before progressing to the next pattern. Finally, much time was invested in seizing, grappling and joint locking.

Sunabako.

75

Sunabako, kami, sashi and chishi.

Training implements of Goju-ryu Karate.

A demonstration of the use of kami.
Note the excellent physical development
produced by this form of training.

"Kobudo"

Modern kami practice.

Yagi Meitoku

The famous Goju-ryu teacher Miyazato Eiichi

Shinjo Masanobu

Uechi-ryu, founded by Uechi Kanbun Sensei. Uechi Sensei traveled to Fukkensho (Fuchou), China where he was schooled in 'Pangai-noon' style. He later settled in Wakayama, Japan where he opened a dojo.

Today, his son, Uechi Kanyei, carries on the proud Uechi-ryu tradition. Uechi Kanyei's son, Uechi Hiroaki, is his heir apparent. Uechi-ryu practitioners are renowned for their impressive physical development. Considerable time is devoted to drills and exercises designed to improve the student's strength and agility. As with Goju-ryu, sanchin training is afforded great importance as are methods of hand conditioning. Kumite is also practiced, sometimes in the form of a contest between opponents. This creates an element of sport which has become one of the main focal points for modern day Japanese Karate training.

Kata include:

    (1)   Sanchin
    (2)   Seshan
    (3)   Sanseryu
    (4)   Kanshiwa
    (5)   Seryu
    (6)   Kanchin
    (7)   Kanshu
    (8)   Sechin

Kobujitsu includes the many, varied methods of defense practiced by Okinawan people that utilize weapons. Some techniques were peculiar to native Okinawans. Others were either influenced by, or imported directly from, China. The kata or series of techniques associated with each weapon were preserved in the same manner as empty hand routines. While styles vary somewhat, there are many common characteristics. The educated observer can discover much by studying similarities, rather than differences.

Uechi Kanei.

Weapons currently still in use.

Bo - a long wood staff.

> A partial list of bo kata:
> (1) Shushi no kon
> (2) Shishi no kon
> (3) Sakugawa no kon
> (4) Shirotaro no kon
> (5) Menta hidaribo
> (6) Sunakake
> (7) Ufugusuku
> (8) Kumibo (Bojutsu I)

Sai - iron trident, generally used in pairs. Police officers often utilized sai in the course of carrying out their duties. Also, a popular weapon in China and the Philippines.

Nunchaku - two sticks, each the length of the practitioner's forearm, connected by string, typically used in pairs.

Tuifa - baton-like sticks, the length of each corresponds to the user's forearm, also include a handle or grip. May have originated in Thailand.

Kama - sickles, also used for agricultural purposes (e.g. grass cutting).

Suruchin - flexible, weighted, rope-like material used for trapping and whipping.

Tinbe - shield used with a variety of hand-held weapons.

Eku - oar, originally used by fishermen and farmers. The eku, or kai, is often viewed as the quintessential Okinawan weapon.

Sansetsukon - three-sectional staff that has its origins in Chinese martial arts.

Kinjo Masakazu (with bo) and his son Kinjo Satoshi (with sai)
practicing bo and sai kumite.

Bo.

Tanbo - short staff, usually 1 1/2 - 4 feet that has a variety of uses, generally used in pairs.

Tetsuko (Tekko) - brass-knuckles that, unlike other weapons, were used strictly for self-defense, likely introduced from mainland Japan by Satsuma.

Tetsuchu - rods with sharpened, tapered tips designed to extend beyond the fist. Believed to be of Chinese origin.

Rochin - spear tip mounted on a short piece of wood, generally, eighteen to twenty-four inches in length.

Kinjo Satoshi performing kata with tuifa.

Suruchin.

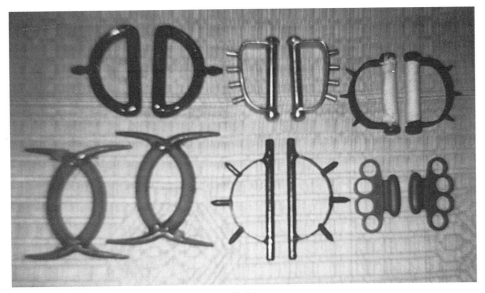

Tekko.

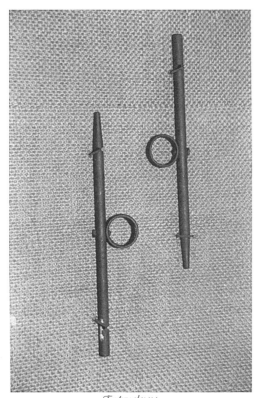

Tetsukyu.

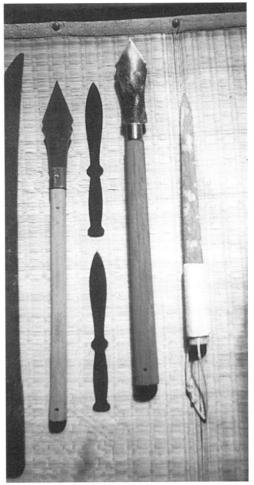

Rochin.

Kiyan Shinei demonstrates the use of the sai.

"Sai."

"Traditional Karate"

Karate and Kobudo's Introduction into the School System

During the Meiji period (1868-1910), the Karate expert, Itosu Anko, presented his book *Toudi Jakkajo* to the Okinawan Prefectural Office. A copy of this text is on display at the Karate Museum in Nishihara. Master Itosu recommended redesigning the school system's fitness program and incorporating martial arts. As a result, a less lethal form of Karate was taught as a compulsory subject for high school students. This shift from self-protection to physical fitness, represented a radical departure from traditional training.

By encouraging youth to learn a traditional native art Itosu Sensei played a pivotal role in further popularizing the study of Karate and ensuring its survival. In a report presented to educational officials, Itosu Sensei outlined some of the key points regarding Karate training.

(1) Karate is a powerful method of self defense.

(2) Karate strengthens both muscles and bones. Therefore, it is logical to begin training at an early age. Use of training implements (e.g. machiwara) and performing techniques from proper stances are essential in developing strength and power.

(3) Three or four years of regular training is required to cultivate a degree of proficiency. School children have the time required to achieve this worthy goal. Conversely, it is harder for an adult to devote themselves in such a manner.

(4) Karate training does not depend on physical strength alone. Even those with physical limitations can gradually develop a high degree of skill and strength.

(5) Karateka usually live for a long time. This is attributable, in large part, to the strengthening of muscle and bone and especially, improved blood circulation.

(6) The degree of concentration required for Karate kata practice exercises the mind. For example, as one trains, one must imagine an opponent's attacks. This prevents distractions from entering the mind.

Itosu's educational aims were logical and well-structured. His proposals, therefore, met with the approval of school authorities. The following summarizes his philosophy with respect to Karate education.

(1) A student should train for at least five years to ensure health benefits.

(2) Recommended advanced kata include Naihanchi, Passai, Kusanku, Chinto and Gojushiho sho.

(3) Five Pinan forms were created with a view to simplifying the type of material practitioners required in order to become more skillful Karateka.

(4) Rules must be established to ensure safety while practicing.

(5) Respect for tradition, proper manners and etiquette are expected of all Karateka.

Initially, Karate was introduced to seven junior high schools.

(1) Okinawa Kenritsu Dai l Junior High School
Hanashiro Chiyoumo taught Karate as the physical education component of this institution's curriculum. Additionally, Itosu Sensei instructed students in their after-school Karate club. The principal kata practiced at this location were Naihanchi, the Pinan series and Passai. Karate was popular among Kenritsu Dai l junior high school students, attributable in large part to the fact

that teachers demonstrated a positive and encouraging style. Further, to promote the concepts of Karate training as an educational tool for the young, this school would often perform demonstrations at local community events.

(2) Kenritsu Danshi Shihan School
This well-respected institution was established in 1980. Karate was introduced into the school's curriculum in 1902 under the guidance of Yabu Kentsu Sensei. Kenritsu Danshi Shihan school students were often asked to demonstrate their skills to dignitaries from mainland Japan. Yabu Sensei taught at this school for twenty-five years before relocating to Hawaii. There, he continued to promote the development of Karate.

(3) Naha Shiritsu Shogyo School
Founded in 1905, this school offered lessons in Karate and Kendo, both of which proved very popular among students. Higaonna Sensei was the Naha Shuritsu Shogyo school's first Karate teacher. He offered lessons there twice a week until his death. He was succeeded by Higaonna's disciple, Miyagi Chojun. Karate became a compulsory subject for students attending this school in 1929.

(4) Kenritsu Kogyo School
Oshiro Chojo introduced Karate and stick fighting techniques at this school, where Judo, Kendo and Karate were required subjects. At a later date, Miyazato Eiichi taught both Karate and Judo.

(5) Kenritsu Dai ll Junior High School
Founded in 1911, this school experienced many problems that necessitated several address and name changes. Murota Sensei served as its Karate teacher throughout these turbulent times. Murota Sensei is a legend in Okinawan Karate circles. He was famous for the amazing strength of his grip and the thickness of the skin on his back, which was reportedly as tough as cowhide.

(6) Kenritsu Norin School
The Sensei at this school, Kyan Chotoku, displayed a special sensitivity for the unique requirements of teaching Karate to youngsters. This likely stemmed from the fact that he, too, had begun training at an early age. Therefore, he understood how best to motivate his young students to train diligently. He demonstrated expert skill in performing the kata Ananku, Passai, Kusanku and Chinto.

(7) Kenritsu Suisan School
Mabuni Sensei was the first to introduce Karate at this school, teaching Suidi and Nahadi styles. The original kata were complex and proved exceptionally difficult to teach in a high school environment. Recognizing this problem, a group of Karateka formed an association in 1941 called the 'Karate-do Senmon Kenkyukai.' The purpose of the 'Student's Study Group'was to promote and

evelop Karate. It was decided that modification of the original kata, to create simplified forms, as necessary. This resulted in the development of Fukyugata 1, created by Nagamine Shoshin nd later Fukyugata 2, introduced by Miyagi Sensei. The value of these forms as martial ducational tools is clearly demonstrated by the fact that they are still practiced at many kinawan Karate schools.

Shinpan Shiroma instructing high school students in front of Shuri castle in 1937.

Miyagi Chojun (seated, 2nd row, 3rd from left) visits the karate club at Naha Commercial High School in 1942.

The author instructing Okinawan high school students.

Classical Versus Modern Training

There was a great deal of debate during the Showa era (1925-1952) concerning the use of protective equipment when practicing kumite. Some University-based Karate schools used protective gear and engaged in free sparring. Conversely, more traditional schools objected strongly to this innovation, arguing that the deadly strikes of Karate were being compromised "watered down," for competition.

In his book *Karate Do Kyohan* Funakoshi Gichin compared Karate to other sports. He concluded that, in terms of being entertaining to spectators, its appeal was limited. To promote "sport" Karate and stimulate interest among spectators and participants, he recommended development of a system for competition. This would include contestants outfitted in protective equipment. At the time Funakoshi penned this book, Karate was pursued as an individual discipline. Although this approach made it unique, it also created obvious obstacles in generating public interest.

Nakamura Shigeru and other noted Okinawan Kenpo experts, supported the use of protective equipment among competitive Karateka.

Funakoshi and Nakamura shared the belief that this concept of "sport" Karate would promote and develop, the martial arts. They were convinced that this would not detract from traditional methods of teaching and learning.

On the subject of kata, most practitioners view it as the heart of any Karate style. It is through diligent practice and innumerable repetitions that kata are learned and understood. Kata challenges the Karateka's body and mind. Each kata should be practiced, analyzed and its applications studied, until the student has grasped its subtleties. At this point, the teacher will introduce another kata and the learning process is repeated.

Personally, I am saddened by the fact that Karate's increased popularity has led to a shift in emphasis from its value as a self-improvement vehicle, to mere sport. This distresses me, as it would appear that this trend may destroy the traditions of Karate and dilute its spiritual power. It has been my observation that as many modern practitioners display an affinity for grandstanding.

Sparring competition at the All Okinawa Karate Championships.

91

Kumite has become more highly valued than kata. I am, therefore, compelled to remin Karateka that kata is the most important element of traditional Okinawan Karate. By repeati kata over and over students train their bodies, as well as their spirits.

The martial arts, steeped in history and strong traditions, have long been tools for person development. The combative styles now boast worldwide awareness. This is attributable, large part, to movies that feature action film stars, like Jackie Chan and Bruce Lee, as well international competitors. It appears that this popularity comes at the expense of spiritu enrichment.

There are however, countless foreigners who have discovered that the study of Okinawan Kara can serve as an invaluable aid in achieving self-actualization. I and other Okinawans believe th Karate forms and purifies the human spirit. As such, its culture and tradition must be careful preserved.

"Karatejutsu"

Karate's Name Change

As noted, the book *Ekkinkyogi* had a profound influence on the martial arts. For example, after the Taisho period (1910-1925), the kanji (characters) used for Shorin-ryu, changed from Karate-do to China hand. It should also be noted that although the prefix characters for Shorin and Shorei are different, both have the same pronunciation.

At the beginning of the 19th century, the kanji symbols for Karate (which translates to China hand) replaced the traditional (Ti). This was an indication of the respect the Okinawan people held for China, the country that had developed martial arts to such a high degree.

In the early 1900's however, people living in mainland Japan, became uncomfortable with the label China. This brought about a new method of writing Karate. In 1905, the first recorded use of this ideogram was made by Hanashiro Chomo, in the publication *Karate Kumite*. Hanshiro was a disciple of Matsumura 'Bushi.' Its use in the mainland was ratified by the Dai Nippon Butokukai in 1933 and three years later, was accepted by the Okinawan martial arts community. The new kanji symbol translated to mean empty hand. This was both spiritually appropriate and politically correct during those turbulent times.

"Karate Do"   *"China Hand"*

93

The Impact of World War II on the Development of Martial Arts

During the Second World War, the development of Karate suffered a great number of setbacks. Many expert Karateka were killed during the fierce battle of Okinawa. Schools and dojos were razed to the ground from the incessant bombing that preceded the landing of American troops. During the American occupation of Japan, all martial activities were banned. In Okinawa, however, practice of Karate was permitted. The occupying forces found it to be similar to Western boxing and therefore, considered it a sport that posed no threat to their security. After the war ended in 1945, the Okinawan people began the daunting task of rebuilding their world which had been brutally devastated. As the schools were rebuilt, students could again study Karate in select locations.

The greatest challenge that existed for Karate's development was the lack of qualified teachers. This problem persisted through the 1940's and 1950's until a new generation of Karateka had been trained to fill the void left after World War II. During the 1960's and 1970's, high school Karate programs became more organized. Governing bodies attempted to unify both the methods of teaching and a system of competition. In 1977, a set of rules was drawn up for high school Karate competition between the mainland and Okinawa. This set the tone for future generations of Karateka.

At present, in Okinawa, one can easily observe stylistic differences between the types of Karate taught in high schools versus traditional dojos. The former, resembles mainland Karate. The latter, is more closely identified with the original, Okinawan method. During the pre-war period and for most of the 1950's and 1960's, Karate instruction was limited to boys. In 1976, however, girls were officially permitted to study the art. Two years later, the Okinawan education authority published the *Karate do Annaisho* (School Karate Guide) which outlined the aims of Karate instruction in the school system. Of paramount interest was the development and preservation of Karate as a unique Okinawan cultural treasure, while recognizing the tremendous health benefits derived from regular martial arts training.

The ruins of Shuri High School photographed
near the end of World War II.

Dissemination of the Martial Arts Internationally

Global diffusion of Karate and Kobudo is vital to the preservation of Budo. This requires the unified efforts of martial arts experts around the world. A significant development was the establishment of the Okinawa Kobudo Kyokai in 1970. This society concluded that while Karate was increasing in popularity, Kobudo was in danger of becoming extinct. In an effort to preserve traditional Kobudo, the society dispatched teachers to foreign countries. Other activities include staging the 'Kobudosai' which is an annual martial arts demonstration in Okinawa. The president of the society, Matayoshi Sensei, is famous throughout the world for his Kobudo expertise. He has devoted his life to promoting traditional Okinawan Kobudo.

Teaching Karate in a foreign country poses numerous challenges to the traditionally- minded Sensei, whose purpose is to promote Okinawan Budo culture. I was fortunate to have interviewed Nakata Sensei who is currently teaching Karate in France. He described some of the difficulties he encountered. These included some lack of receptiveness to foreigners, inability to communicate in a common language and elaborate visa requirements. Additionally, he recounted cultural differences, which involved students who were more inclined than their Japanese counterparts to question teaching methods and techniques.

(1) As the martial arts are no longer considered secret, teachers have become more receptive to sharing information when instructing visitors to Okinawa.

(2) The martial arts have been showcased globally through demonstrations and tournaments. Competitive events are enjoying rising popularity, attributable, in some degree, to the use of protective equipment.

(3) The martial arts enjoy popularity as a form of entertainment. Audiences, even non-practitioners, can understand and enjoy their aestheticism and athleticism.

(4) There has been a tremendous surge of interest in all things oriental. As a result, there is a worldwide, well-educated audience for martial arts and their heritage.

*Ken Shi Kai students performing Sanchin at
the 1995 "Kobudosai" event in Okinawa.*

(5) Martial arts training has been found to be of exceptional benefit to the preservation of good health. This is a common desire that transcends national and cultural boundaries.

(6) The martial arts fortify the spirit in ways that no other discipline, or sport can achieve. Practitioners around the world recognize this benefit and search tirelessly for any information that may enhance their development.

(7) Museums and institutions have been established to educate the public, as well as martial arts practitioners, regardless of discipline, style, or national origin.

The Okinawan government has approved funding for a Karate and Kobudo information centre where visitors can learn more about this unique Okinawan phenomenon. I shall continue to devote my energies to this most worthwhile endeavour.

Tentative exhibits include the History of Karate and Kobudo, an overview, Introduction to Karate, includes training implements and methods of use. Introduction to Kobudo, tools Introduction to Karate and Kobudo experts, demonstrations by Karate and Kobudo experts and a library with a variety of print and audiovisual aids.

Through these institutions, the efforts of dedicated teachers, international events and publications, films and videotapes, we will better understand our chosen martial arts, as well as Okinawan culture as a whole.

(Editor's note: With respect to this last tactic, the author has built the Okinawan Prefectural Karate and Kobudo Museum. This institution serves as a home for Hokama Sensei's remarkable collection of martial arts memorabilia and cultural artifacts. It is opened to the public in order that others may share the wealth of knowledge that he has accumulted through his years of research and study. It is Hokama Sensei's sincere hope that the Okinawan government will recognize the importance of his collection and assist him in developing this veritable treasure trove. This will enable visitors to more fully understand the traditions and rich heritage, of this beautiful island. It will also afford them the opportunity to appreciate the significant contribution the Okinawan people have made to the development of the martial arts.)

Kent Moyer with his wife Kaoru Moyer.

96

"World Peace Through Karate Do"

Assorted nunchaku on display at the Okinawa Prefectural Museum. At top right, a traditional nunchaku that evolved from a horse bridle.

双節棍の変遷

古武道

拳行八筆呑

Double handled tuifa photographed at the Okinawa Prefectural Museum imported from Thailand with traditional Okinawan variey.

The Museum's tribute to famous Okinawan dance teachers.

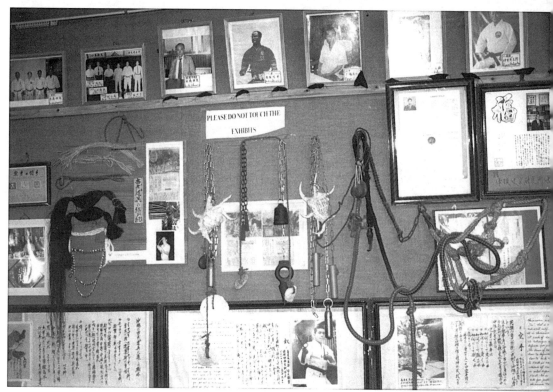

Collection of suruchin housed at the Okinawa Prefectural Museum.

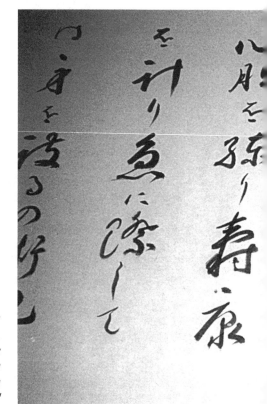

Miyagi Sensei's karate teachings:
"What is Karate? You don't carry a weapon.
Its use during times of peace is to train the
spirit as well as the body. This will bring
good health and a long life. In an emergency
you can respond without hesitation."

Future Growth of the Martial Arts

The philosophy of the martial arts, advises us that we should only use our skills in self-defense. This is an ancient lesson that has been handed down to each generation. It is the hope of all martial arts instructors that by teaching and spreading the knowledge of Karate and Kobudo, we will produce peace in the world. This, too, is my sincere wish and my purpose in writing this book.

The future of the martial arts depends on qualified teachers transmitting the techniques and culture to practitioners throughout the world. There is a strong connection between educational institutions and the art of Karate. Most educators agree that Karate training has a beneficial influence on students, from junior high to University level. The discipline of the art enriches the practitioner's life, thereby producing self-disciplined and conscientious students.

On a grand scale, one can only imagine how these benefits could be magnified through formation of several schools, or Universities, whose primary focus is the culture and traditions of the martial arts - like the Kokusai Budo University in Chiba, Japan.

At this institution, future teachers receive a comprehensive education that is not limited to martial arts (e.g. Judo and Kendo are compulsory subjects). Rather, the program also includes foreign languages and cultural studies. This will equip them with the skills necessary to foster mutual understanding and promote peace between nations.

Authorities are also exploring the feasibility of opening the Okinawa-Kenritsu Geijitsu University, which will place primary emphasis on Okinawan culture. The curriculum would include Ryukyuan history, literature, music and dance.

It is my fervent desire that Karate will also be included in the syllabus of these Universities as a compulsory subject.

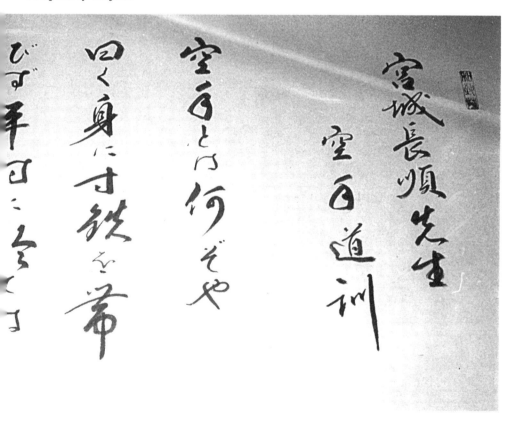

"Tan Den"

TRAINING GUIDE
SECTION 1

EXCERPTS FROM EKKINKYOGI

Part One: Ekkin kyogi

The two elements of mind and body are both equally important. They must be trained and disciplined to ensure correct development. In this way, an individual can reach maximum potential. Those who study 'Butsujo' and follow the teachings of Buddha, must be familiar with two words and their applications. 'Seikyo,' which relates to the spiritual and 'Ekikyo,' which relates to the physical. The concept of Seikyo is addressed in the book of 'Senzuikyo.' Ekikyo is described in 'Ekkinkyo.'

To describe Seikyo one can say that - if the heart is clean, you will meet with no obstacles in life. The concept being the "washing" or purification of one's heart - a literal translation would be "marrow washing."

Ekikyo says - if you have courage, your trials will go well. This refers to training the muscles and strengthening the body or more literally, "sinew changing."

The human body is held together by muscles. If the muscles become loose, the body becomes painful. If the muscles tighten, the body becomes misshapen and bent. On the other hand, if the muscles are developed and kept in good condition, the health of the individual will be exceptionally good. This is a God-given, natural function of the body. Anyone who has a strong will, patience and fortitude will be able to achieve self-improvement in this way.

Part Two: Kiko-inner power

- To develop Kiko, it is very important to use the proper method of breathing. One must pay special attention to correct posture, sitting with the back straight. Look directly ahead and keep the mouth relaxed, rather than tightly shut.

- Do not practice Kiko when there is a strong wind, heavy rain or thunder. These are signs of the anger of the heavens. Practice only when the weather is calm and the results will be beneficial.

- Kiko should be practiced three times a day, once at 6 a.m., once at noon and once at 6 p.m. It is not recommended to practice twice or four times a day. Practice everyday, on an empty stomach, in a well-ventilated room.

- If you are feeling tired or weak, you can revive yourself by practicing Kiko. It will invigorate both your body and your spirit.

- You will not need to use medicines if you practice Kiko. It affects your internal chemistry, making the body resistant to disease and infection.

- Do not use power to practice Kiko. You should feel relaxed and practice in a natural way.

- When you begin Kiko training, it is advised that you do not drink alcohol at all for the first three months. After this abstinence period, you may drink moderately, without affecting your health. Those with a delicate constitution however, should refrain from drinking altogether.

- Kiko can, and should be, practiced by everyone - men, women, old and young. The elderly will rejuvenate themselves through its practice and women will find childbirth much easier.

- Use the "method of breathing" seven times daily for ten days. Then, add 'Bukoto shiki' (which is a type of Kiko method) to the right and left sides and reduce the "method of breathing" to six times. After ten more days, add "Fukuiza shiki' to the right and left, three times each. Additionally, perform the "method of breathing" six times. Again, after ten days add 'Kosho shiki' to the right and left, along with the "method of breathing" six times. Continue in this way for a total of eight days. Then commence 'Dako,' or striking training.

- The principal tool of Dako involves the use of a small cloth bag. The bag contains 'awa,' which looks and feels like rice. The awa is put in the bag, which is traditionally indigo blue and it is tied shut. Do not overfill the bag, as the empty section should be used as a handle for striking.

- To practice Dako, begin on the left side of the body, hitting shoulder, elbow and hand in that order. Continue with the side, from armpit, to belly to feet. Then, proceed to twenty strikes on the left side of the back. Take a bag in your right hand and hit your lower back on the left side. The same procedure should then be carried out on the right side of the body. The correct sequence of strikes is essential. If one sequence is omitted, do not go back to it. Simply continue with the sequence you started until it is complete. Every time you strike, you must use the "method of breathing" once.

Although, it requires sixty-five executions of the method of breathing to complete the Dako system. It should be practiced for one year. At this point, 'Junte nana shiki' should be added for ten days, using the "method of breathing" four times. Then, the 'Hentei shiki' can be practiced with the "method of breathing" nine times. Next, 'Bukoko shiki' and 'Retsu hiza shiki' are practiced for ten days each, using the "method of breathing" - three and six times, respectively. In all, the "method of breathing" will be practiced eighty-seven times, which brings the first step of Kiko to completion.

- If you complete Kiko's first step, your spirit will become lively and you will experience increased energy levels. To finish all four steps of the Kiko method, it takes two years. During this time, your body will become strong and vigorous. According to legend, if you complete Kiko, you will be able to pierce the stomach of a cow with two fingers and break its neck with the side of your hand. In addition to these feats of strength, your life span will also be greatly extended.

- If you hand it down you don't have to write it down - this refers to the important role played by oral tradition.

Part Three: Senzui Kyogi

People who wish to prolong their lives even further, should practice 'Senzui' after they complete 'Ekkin.' This is the direction stated in the book Joya no kane, which addresses the trails of the human condition. People spend most of their waking hours dealing with basic needs like food and shelter. They forget life and death only when they sleep. Death will inevitably come to us all and it is through 'Senzui' that the duration and quality of life can be improved.

To practice, sit down and close your eyes. Breathe silently through the nose. This peaceful practice should be conducted at noon and midnight and again at 6 a.m. and 6 p.m. on the first and last day of each month. This should also be done the night of the harvest moon, the vernal and autumnal equinox and the summer and winter solstice. If you train your spirit diligently, you will not get sleepy. Avoid overeating, maintain a healthy lifestyle and keep your body strong.

TRAINING GUIDE
SECTION 2

TECHNIQUES AND APPLICATIONS OF KAPPO

The following are eight Kappo techniques.

(1) Jokatsu Kokyuho

Two people are needed to perform this technique of artificial respiration. The unconcious patient should be lain flat on his back and one of the people should position themselves by the head of the patient. Taking the patient by the arms, the hands are moved upwards towards the head and then back down to the sides. The second attendant kneels close to the side of the body, placing both palms on the patient's lower stomach. The two attendants work in sequence. When the patient's arms are lifted towards their head, the second attendant pushes gently upward toward the chest. Once the hands are returned to the patient's side, the pressure should be released. This technique should be performed fifteen to twenty times per minute, until the patient begins to breathe without assistance.

A variation of this technique involves the second attendant holding the patient's ankles while bending and extending the legs, as the other attendant moves the patient's arms. The purpose of this technique is to force fresh air into the lungs. This may stimulate the patient to resume natural breathing. If the patient's mouth is closed, tilt the head back by lifting the chin. This will provide a clear passageway for air. If only one person is available to assist the patient, they should place a pillow under the patient's back and move the arms up and down as previously described. It may take some time for this technique to work, so do not give up too quickly.

(2) Haikatsu Yudoho

This technique can be performed alone by placing yourself in a seated position with the patient's head in front of you. Slide your hands under the patient's armpits and raise him up to a seated position supported by your legs. Take your left hand from under the armpit and turn his chin toward his left shoulder. Withdraw your right hand from under the armpit and reach over his right shoulder. Again, grip him under the armpit, but this time, from the front. While still supporting his back with your left leg, place your right foot in the centre of his back. Push gently while pulling with your hands. Synchronize the pushing and pulling motions with your own natural breathing. Repeat two, or three times. If you need to move the body, do so by replacing your hands under the armpits from behind, as described in the opening position.

Professor Wally Jay demonstrates Kappo revival techniques.

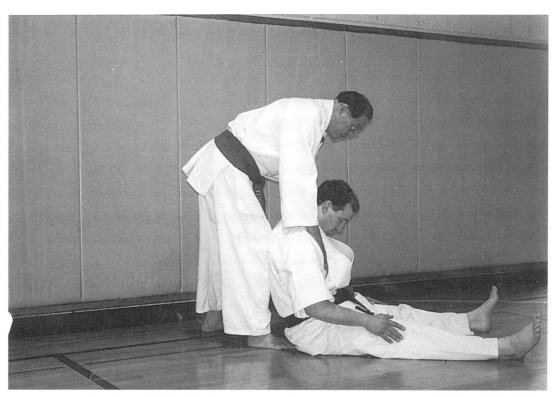

Professor Wally Jay demonstrates Kappo revival techniques.

(3) Kin Kappatsu Shinpo

The aim of this technique is to send a vibration through the body. This may stimulate the nervous system, the heart and lungs, in an effort to restore natural breathing. Raise the body to a seated position. Slide your hands under his armpits from behind, as described in Haikatsu Yudoho above. Kneel on your right knee with his back lying against your chest. Your left leg supports his left side, thereby preventing him from falling. With your left hand, support his chin, so that his head is immobilized. Place your right palm flat against his spine with your index finger on the backbone. Take a deep breath and as you exhale, firmly strike the patient's back with the heel of your palm. The shock should restore his natural breathing pattern.

(4) Haikatsu Kyukiho

Lie the patient face down and turn his head to the side. Kneel astride the patient, but avoid putting too much pressure on his body. Use your palms to stroke him, from shoulder to waist serveral times, with a gentle, yet firm, touch. Locate the ninth vertebrae and place the heel of both your palms on either side of the spine. Using a strong pushing motion, apply pressure briefly and immediately release it. Repeat this movement several times, until the patient begins to breathe independently. It is important to release the pressure immediately after you push, as continued downward tension may impede the breathing reflex.

(5) Sokatsu Kikaiho

To perform this technique, the patient should be carefully placed on his back on the floor. Kneel astride the body. Avoid putting any pressure on him by putting your left knee against his right thigh and your right foot on the ground close to his chest. Use your palms to stroke his body from shoulders to stomach several times. Cup your left hand under his neck and raise his head at the same time. Immediately release the pressure with both hands and repeat in a natural breathing rhythm. The key factor here is to perform the technique quickly and to coordinate the pressure of both hands.

Professor Wally Jay demonstrates Kappo revival techniques.

(6) Kokatsu Kashoho

This technique is used to treat a patient who has been injured by a blow to the testicles. Raise the patient by lifting him under the armpits until his legs are straight. Use the sole of the foot to kick him at the base of the spine. If you do not strike too hard, you can kick several times without risk of injury to the patient. The testicles should drop down to a natural position. If this technique is unsuccessful, Haikatsu Yudoho and Sokatsu Kikaiho technique should be applied.

(7) Suikatsu Tosuiho

This technique is to be used for victims of drowning. After clearing their nose and mouth of any mucous or obstacles to breathing, place something soft under the middle of his back to raise the chest. One attendant should tilt the patient's face upward, while a second person pushes against the stomach with their palms. Repeating this motion several times will cause the patient to expel the water they have swallowed. Once this is accomplished, perform technique number four to revive the patient completely. If you have to perform this technique alone, then you must place the patient with his head tilted to his right. Ensure his tongue is not obstructing his throat. Push slowly, but firmly, for about two seconds against his stomach. Then, gradually release the pressure. Repeat this action until water is expelled and natural breathing resumes.

An alternative method is to place a pillow under the patient's stomach. Apply pressure to his back with your palms to expel the water swallowed during drowning. Complete the treatment with another Kappo technique to regulate breathing.

(8) Sokatsu Seigyoho

This is a revival technique for a person who has been hanged. While it can be performed alone, it is far safer when two people are available. Place a support under the feet of the hanging body and lift under the armpits from behind. The second person should then cut the rope, taking care not to allow the patient's neck to move suddenly. Lie him down on a soft surface, such as

Professor Wally Jay demonstrates Kappo revival techniques.

clothing or blankets. The manner of taking the body down is critical. Any rough vibration will reduce the chances of revival significantly. If the victim has been hanging only a short time, then Kin Kappatsu Shinpo should be attempted. If a long period of time has elapsed, it will be more advisable to administer Sokatsu Kikaiho.

The eight techniques described above can produce seemingly miraculous results. We are advised that if one of these methods is not successful, then we should try another Kappo technique. If the patient has been unconscious for a long period, or if they are the victim of a severe blow to the head, you should use a feather to tickle the nose or throat. This should produce a sneezing, or coughing reflex that may stimulate a breathing response. Another option is a technique called 'Shindenno Kakki Shinpo.' Working with the body lying on it back, raise the patient to a seated position by lifting under the armpits from behind. Move to the right side of the body. Kneel so that you can support his back with your left leg. Press your right fingertips against his temples and your left fingertips against the back of his head. Apply equal pressure with both hands and press toward the centre of the head. Maintain steady pressure for fifteen to thirty seconds. Relax and then re-apply pressure for another fifteen to thirty seconds before trying for a second time. This technique can be attempted several times without risk to the patient.

A Kappo technique known as 'Shinden Tokatsu Junbiho' is self-administered. It is intended to protect oneself from injury, as well as concentrating the spirit and ridding the mind of fear. Many practitioners use this technique as a form of protection before a sparring match. Assume a seated meditation posture with your toes overlapping. Place your hands at your side and with your back straight, inhale deeply. Hold your breath for a while and each time you exhale, chant the following nine words; (Jumon) Rin Hei To Sha Kai Jin Retsu Zai Zen. As you chant each word, focus your energy into the tanden (pit of your stomach) for one second. Relax for one second before chanting the next syllable. Perform this technique nine times. Repeat the process with your legs, fists and chest focusing energy into the tanden. Once you've finished, place a pinch of salt on your tongue. The protective power of this technique will last for four hours.

This is a form of 'Kototama,' or martial arts chants, a secretive, highly advanced method of spiritual fortification.

TRAINING GUIDE
SECTION 3

KENPO TRAINING METHOD FOR CONSIDERATION

In ancient times, metaphors for the human body and nature were common. For example, water falling constantly will wear down a stone. In the same way, we must train the human body through consistent daily effort. The seemingly impossible can be achieved through diligence. Humans have blood circulating through their veins. This explains why they are affected by changes in the weather, such as seasonal variations of humidity and other meteorological factors.

Kenpo speaks of breath inhalation as 'ju' and 'go' - the exhaled breath. Karate depends on this harmony of breathing. It becomes vitally important during combat.

When fighting, you can create an advantage by destroying your opponent's concentration. By learning Budo, you can judge the opponent's actions through sensitivity to movement and sound. Maintaining a hightened level of concentration will enable you to read your opponent's intentions.

Methods of conditioning the hands and striking techniques follow.

Tetsusa no te (iron palm).
Sand and stones should be heated and repeatedly struck with the fist. The fingertips can be conditioned using pieces of bamboo bundled together. This method of training will change the shape of the fingers and often the fingernails drop off, leaving a hard, calloused surface.

Various types of sunabako used for hand conditioning.

Ichiroso waza no te

This technique uses the forefinger to strike and requires special conditioning. If you are hit from behind with this technique, you will feel the attack as a strong percussive blow. The result of the strike, however, are delayed. The intention of this technique is to traumatise the internal organs. This will result in dysfunction and illness, or death.

Kanran no te (sea-horse hand)

An attack using this technique to the head, or spine, will create a blockage in the brain. To treat this injury, apply cold water to the point of injury and lower your head below the level of your heart.

Kotento no te

This technique is used to attack the vital point between the ribs. It is an effective technique which shocks the opponent and causes them to lose consciousness.

Seven life-threatening vital points:

The following seven life-threatening vital points should be avoided, unless the intention is to kill one's opponent.

Head. The most important part of the body. Techniques directed at this area are potentially lethal and should be considered carefully. Attacking the top of the head can result in unconsicousness, or death.

Back of the head. An extremely sensitive area. A blow to the neck will result in paralysis and breathing my cease.

Back of the ears. An area that can be attacked to produce excruciating pain and loss of consciousness. As with all of these vital points, extreme force can kill the recipient of the technique.

Throat. Study the vital point where the collarbones meet. Striking this cavity will cause the person to choke and their breathing will be impaired sufficiently to cause death.

Sides of the body at the floating rib area. Can be struck, effectively shutting down the nervous system. The victim may vomit blood before losing consciousness and dying.

Testicles. An extremely vulnerable part of the male anatomy. A strong blow to the testicles will cause an inability to breathe and eventually - death.

Chest. An interesting target area, especially at the left side above the heart. Striking this point will damage the internal organs, which in turn causes the victim to lose consciousness.

When someone has been injured by a sword, spear or a gun, the results are usually fatal, especially if the wound becomes infected. Medicine is usually of no help once the body's temperature drops. It is a signal that death is imminent. If the eyes are without movement, the system has shut down and death is inevitable. (See also Section 2 - Techniques and Applications of Kappo.)

An interesting symbolic representation of the body's vital points can be found in Buddhist structures called 'Gorinto' (five ring tower). Five different shapes are assembled in a particular sequence, from bottom to top; a square, a circle, a triangle, a half moon and an oval. The lowest stone, the square, is closest to the ground. It represents the lower body. The circle represents water, hence the stomach. The triangle symbolizes fire, or the heart. The half-moon stands for wind and the face. Finally, the oval signifies the sky, or the head, in anatomical terms.

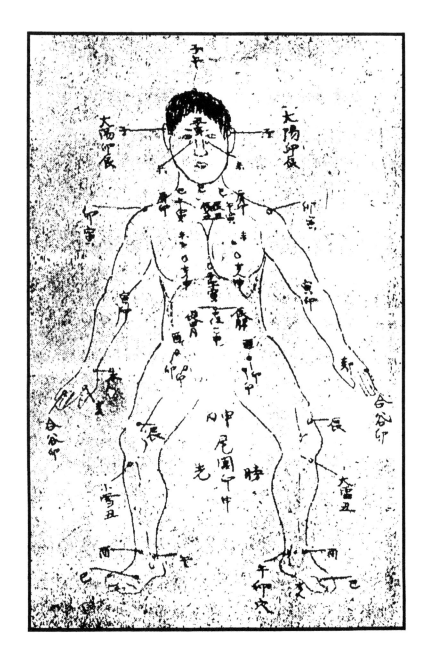

(1)   (2)

The author demonstrates Seisan kata.

(5)   (6)

(3)

(4)

(7)

(8)

(9)

(10)

(13)

(14)

(11)

(12)

(15)

(16)

(17)

(18)

(21)

(22)

(19)

(20)

(23)

(24)

(25)

(26)

(29)

(30)

(27)

(28)

(31)

(32)

(33)

(34)

(37)

(38)

(35)

(36)

(39)

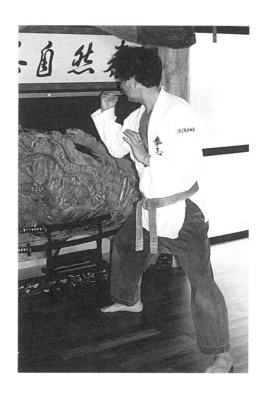

(40)

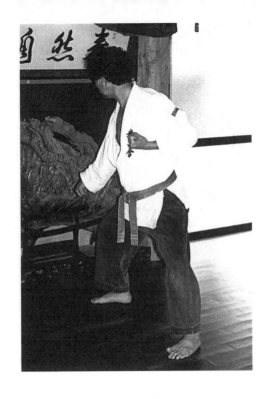

(41)

(42)

(45)

(46)

(43)   (44)

(47)   (48)

(49)

(50)

(53)

(54)

(51)   (52)

TRAINING GUIDE
SECTION 4

KAKIE

Kakie is practiced in pairs. It involves participants endeavouring to overcome their partner through pushing and pulling, unbalancing and striking. The object of the excercise is to explore different techniques of attack and defense. It emphasizes the importance of breath control. It requires a deep understanding of how to both exert and yield, to force.

In Kakie practice, when your opponent pushes hard, you must react softly. This will enable you to redirect the attacker's energy - effectively using their own power against themselves.

Watching Goju-ryu stylists practicing Kakie, one is reminded of Tai Chi's "push hands." The apparent gentleness of the movements masks the explosive power generated through correct body management and awareness of your attacker's centre of gravity. An important aspect of this "soft" method of defense, are seizing of nerve points and joint locks. These are implied, but not necessarily clearly illustrated, in everyday practice of such systems.

(1)   (2)

Kakie drill (basic).

(5)   (6)

(3)   (4)

(1)   (2)

Kakie drill (Palm Heel Strike).

(5)   (6)

(3)

(4)

(1)

(2)

Kakie drill (Elbow Strike).

(5)

(6)

(3)

(4)

"Bu"   "Dance"

TRAINING GUIDE
SECTION 5

TI AND DANCE

The following photographs illustrate the relationship between native combative techniques - Ti and Okinawan folkdance.

(1)

(2)

Ti and Okinawan dance demonstration.

(5)

(6)

138

(3)

(4)

(7)

(1)   *(2)*

Ti and Okinawan dance demonstration.

(5)   *(6)*

(3)   (4)

(1)   (2)

Ti and Okinawan dance demonstration.

(5)   (6)

(3)

(4)

(7)

(1)   (2)

Ti and Okinawan dance demonstration.

(5)   (6)

(3)

(4)

(7)

(8)

(1) (2)

Ti and Okinawan dance demonstration.

(5) (6)

(3)

(4)

(7)

(1)

(2)

Ti and Okinawan dance demonstration.

(5)

(6)

(3)   (4)

Martial Arts Accomplishments of Tetsuhiro Hokama.

1952 - learned Karate fundamentals from grandfather Tokuyama Seiken
1961 - formal martial arts education commenced, Karate club, Naha Commercial High School
- began training with Higa Seiko
1964 - Vice-President, Karate-do Club, Chiba Commercial University
1966 - enrolled in Fukuchi Seiko Dojo, following the death of Master Higa
1967 - established Karate Club at Okinawa-Ken Student Hall
1970 - launched Goju-ryu Club at Miyako High School and served as instructor
1971 - launched Goju-ryu Club at Hentona High School and served as instructor
- created High School Sports Association (Northern Okinawa branch)
- directed High School Karate-do Tournament
1974 - Director of Okinawa High School Karate-do Association
1976 - instructor of Chubu Commercial High School
1977 - awarded title of Shihan in Goju-ryu
1978 - performed at Meiji Shrine, 25th Memorial Celebration honouring Miyagi Chojun
1979 - referee at the All Okinawa Karate Do Championship
1981 - technical advisor at the All Japan Karate-do Ken Yu Kai
- demonstrator at the International Karate-do Championships
- First Secretary at the All Okinawa Karate-do Association
1983 - conducted seminars in England and France
- featured in Fighting Arts magazine
- special guest at the 30th Anniversary High School Sports Association
- performer and referee at the All Okianwa Karate-do championships
- instructor in Goju-ryu, Nanbu Commercial High School
1984 - published *History of Okinawan Karate-do*
- published *Karatedo* in schools
1985 - Chief, Sports and Welfare Division, Okinawa Department of Education
- Okinawan representative, Chinese-Okinawan Martial Exchange Tournament
1986 - lecturer, Karate and Kobudo, Okinawa Development Bank Hall
1987 - lecturer, Karate and Kobudo, Nanbu Commercial High School
1988 - established Okinawa Karate and Kobudo Historical Museum
1989 - conducted seminars in England
- published *Okinawan Ancient Martial Arts Tools*
- organizer, Ken Shi kai 10th Anniversary Tournament
1990 - conducted study of Chinese Kenpo   (Shokakuken) in Taiwan
- President, Nishihara Machi Cultural Association
- conducted seminars in South Africa
- member of the World Uchinanchu Kai
1991 - appointed researcher (Kobudo) by Okinawan Government
1992 - published calligraphy book on Okinawan proverbs
- conducted seminars in Finland
1993 - received a special commendation from the U.S. Senate for promoting Karate in the United States
- lecturer, 42nd Kyushu Sports Meeting
- received special award from the Finnish Army for promoting Karate in Europe
- demonstrator, 27th All Japan Women's Congress
present - researching and writing articles and books on a variety of martial arts and related topics, including 'Village Stick Combat' a study commissioned by the Okinawan Department of Education.

Non-Martial Arts Accomplishments of Tetsuhiro Hokama.

- Master, Shungan Calligraphy
- member, Japan Calligraphy Association
- instructor, Japan Calligraphy School

- Master, Okinawa's Mineral and Stone Research Association
- research scholar, Okinawa Familty Crest Study Group
- representative, Nishihara Machi Cultural Association